St.Joseph
A Pictorial History

by
Mildred Grenier

STOCK YARDS & LAKE CONTRARY

Design by
Jamie Backus-Raynor

Donning Company/Publishers
Virginia Beach/Norfolk

To Joe

ISBN 0-89865-141-7

Printed in the United States of America

Contents

Foreword

Mildred Grenier has given St. Joseph a gift. It is a gift of pictorially recording its history from the native Americans of the late 1700s to the new Americans of the 1980s. In more than 350 pictures we see our town grow from Blacksnake Hills Trading Post to St. Joseph—college town, agricultural center, industrial center, and a good place to live.

She has gathered her pictures from various sources. Some are familiar and well-known pictures while others are shown here publicly for the first time. All are carefully arranged and combined with text to bring history to life.

The presence of the Missouri River is about the only constant in an ever-changing town. It, too, assumes a changing character. Here we see the quiet river and bluffs of Joseph Robidoux, the busy river of the steamboat captains, the untamed river of the flood of '52, and the Corp-controlled river flowing alongside I-229.

People who made St. Joseph important are in Mrs. Grenier's book. Famous people—Joseph Robidoux, Chief White Cloud, Jeff Thompson, Johnny Fry. Jesse James, St. Joseph's three Missouri governors, and Eugene Field—are all here. Also here are the unnamed but equally important people—seamstresses at the Englehart-Davison Company, trolley car conductors and passengers, schoolchildren of the 1880s, the 1875 fire department, and the participants of the first Pony Express rerun.

Recorded are the buildings forever gone to St. Joseph. There is the Kay home in what is now the heart of downtown St. Joseph. Union Station, the first high school, Hotel Robidoux, early Krug Park, and many other landmarks still exist in pictures. Through pictures one can see the growth of the town to the east and the development of Missouri Western State College.

St. Joseph citizens are shown at play—men boxing and college girls playing basketball. The circus comes to town as does Jack Benny. Children play in Krug Park and musicians join Rosenblatt's Band of the late 1860s. The New Era Exposition of 1889, before being destroyed by fire, raises St. Joseph's hopes of attracting a world's fair.

Work is important to St. Joseph. Men are shown collecting tolls on the Iron Bridge in 1875, cleaning cattle at the Krug Packing Company, making the driveways through Krug Park in the 1930s, and sandbagging the Missouri River in 1952.

Pictures show St. Joseph reacting to world events around it: the Pawpaw Militia of the Civil War, War Dads feeding trainloads of soldiers in the 1940s, the World War I flag display, the welcome of Charles Lindbergh, Truman's campaign during a whistle stop—all are here.

Saint Joseph: A Pictorial History is a delightful way to relive St. Joseph's past in two or three hours of pure enjoyment.

Jacqueline Lewin
Curator of History
St. Joseph Museum

9

Preface

St. Joseph has always been known as a friendly city—"Where Southern Hospitality mingles with the Democracy of the West." Its churches are called hospitable, its clubs called cordial, its businesses called accommodating and affable. However, I never fully appreciated the extent of this strong sense of community until I began to research material and to collect photographs for this book. Family members willingly dug through dusty trunks and boxes in attics and basements; busy city and county officials generously shared guarded records, yellowed and crackling with age; librarians gave unstintingly of their time; church and school directors went far beyond the call of duty to be helpful.

In the genesis of our town, as in almost all towns, I suppose, people were sometimes too busy making history to take time to sit down and record it, so specific dates and locations are sometimes impossible to pinpoint. Many sources of information were consulted in the preparation of this book, and when conflicting information appeared, I used as my guide dates or other facts most frequently found.

This book is not intended as a scholarly work. It is meant to be an informative and entertaining essay which captures the flavor of major transitions in community life and presents a comprehensive view of the city's evolution from earliest-known information to current developments.

The overall picture that evolves is a colorful montage of many textures, sights, and sounds—the paths of deer searching out salt licks, a bark canoe cutting a swift, sure path up a river, covered wagon trails winding through tall prairie grass and Indian paintbrush, to modern, five-lane interstates... the howl of a wolf around a lonely log cabin, the sound of a fiddle, lowing of cattle in feedlots, noon factory whistles, to the music of modern symphonies... the clang of the blacksmith anviling out the hoofbeats of history, the wail of the steamboats, the rhythmic clank of steel on steel, to the silent white streaks of today's jets busily stitching our country together...

St. Joseph's ancestors who had a hand in painting the picture were strong men and women. Men like Joseph Robidoux, who as a boy of sixteen fearlessly pushed into an untrodden wilderness to blaze the way not only for a new town but for a new nation as well... men like Logan James, who came to Washington Township in 1838 and split 2,500 rails to buy his first cow... men like Reverend Reeves, who shouldered an axe with the rest of his small congregation to build the first log church in St. Joseph, and his wife who lived in a stable and, with pots, kettles, and skillets in a rude fireplace in a chimney composed of mud and sticks, cooked dinner for the working men and carried it to them at noon. A city with this ancestry is resting on a firm foundation.

It is impossible for me to name all the people who helped me compile this book, and for that I am sorry. I was fortunate to have the help of four top photographers in this city—Don Reynolds of the St. Joseph and Pony Express Stables Museums; Mike Wylie of Strathmann Photography; Wesley Hazelwood of Ziph Photography, and Ival Lawhon, Jr., of the *St. Joseph News-Press* and *Gazette* staff. Richard Nolf, Director of the St. Joseph Museum, Jacqueline Lewin, Curator of History, and Don Reynolds generously shared their records and knowledge of St. Joseph history, helped me identify many pictures and loaned their photographs. These pictures are among the hundreds taken by Don Reynolds and are housed in the St. Joseph Museum.

Dorothy Elliot, Director of St. Joseph Public Library, gave me unqualified access to the library's holdings; Doris Finley, Head Librarian, and her dedicated staff kindly assisted me in the selection and location of many photographs. The director and staff of the Missouri Western State College similarly offered assistance and open admission to their extensive collections and to the graphics department files of *The Griffon* yearbooks. Frank Popplewell shared his knowledge of the college history, and Sheridan Logan, well-known historian and author, contributed facts concerning St. Joseph history.

David R. Bradley, Jr., managing editor of the *St. Joseph News-Press*, granted me access to the newspaper's files. Jim Ray, Director of the Albrecht Art Museum, gave permission to reproduce many of the art museum's outstanding photographs.

Further help was given me by Buchanan County Recorder Thomas Sloan, Barry Claywell and Robert Slater of the St. Joseph Light and Power Company, Robert Starks of the St. Joseph Fire Department, and Harold Cole, manager of the St. Joseph Water Company.

I am also indebted to the members of St. Joseph's three historical societies, particularly to Roy Coy of the Pony Express Historical Association, Mary Boder of the St. Joseph Historical Society, and Louis Parmelee of the Buchanan County Historical Society.

chapter 1

Native Americans

Ten thousand years ago, the climate in this part of the country was cool and moist, and vegetation was lush. As the climate became warmer and drier, ice age mammals and certain species of vegetation disappeared, and man increased in numbers. Many Indian tribes migrated into this section. It is not yet clear whether the Missouri or Kansas tribe was the earliest here. Later, the Otoe, Iowa, Sauk, and Fox tribes became the greatest in number.

In 1820, the Iowa Indians had a large village on the Blacksnake Creek just three miles north of St. Joseph. This tribe of Indians, described as excellent examples of ideal physical types, was led by Chief White Cloud, a very intelligent and outstanding warrior (Roy Coy, *St. Joseph Museum Graphic*).

In 1824, the government ceded to the Indians all the land along the Missouri River from Platte County on the south to the Iowa border on the north. The white man wanted the fertile land and began to move in. The Indians retaliated and there were fights. William Clark of Lewis and Clark fame was the Superintendent of Indian Affairs. September 17, 1836, he negotiated a treaty with the Iowa, Sauk, and Fox tribes which gave the Indians 400 sections of land in what is now Kansas, $7,500, five homes, and 200 acres of land for the Iowas, and furnished them with a farmer, schoolmaster, blacksmith, interpreter, agricultural implements, a ferry boat, rations, a mill, and livestock. In return, the Indians, after seeking guidance from the Great Spirit, gave the white man the Platte country, the land where the bones of their ancestors lay (Hazel Faubion, *Tales of Old "St. Joe" and the Frontier Days*).

Copy of a painting made at Blacksnake Creek, St. Joseph, 1848, by Rudolph F. Kurz. Photograph courtesy of the St. Joseph Museum

King Hill as it once was before the coming of white settlers. The Missouri River is to the right. The Indians in and around St. Joseph became mound builders and placed their dead in mounds on top of the many bluffs in this city. King Hill was the sacred burial hill of the Missouri Indians, and it was later a landmark for the early explorers and fur traders coming up the river named for these Indians. It no doubt was the center of a large village or of numerous small villages in this area (Roy Coy, St. Joseph Museum Graphic). Photograph courtesy of the St. Joseph Museum

Native Americans

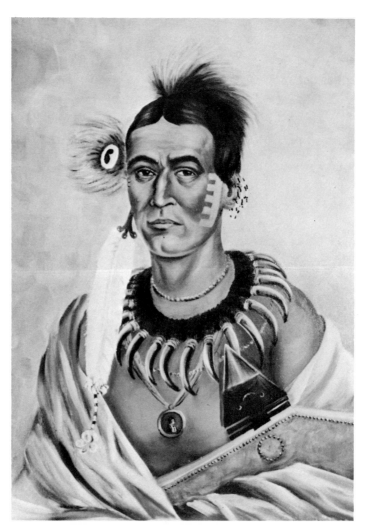

Chief White Cloud, chief of the Iowas, about 1824. Photograph courtesy of the St. Joseph Museum and Strathmann Photography

This picture is thought to be a self-portrait of Rudolph Frederick Kurz, made August 26, 1851. Kurz, a noted Swiss artist, spent more than two years in St. Joseph in the 1840s and 1850s and made a number of the sketches shown on these pages. Many of the sketches are not finished, but they give some idea of the life-style of the local Indians of that period. Photograph courtesy of the St. Joseph Museum

Finished painting of the Pottawa-
tomie Indians at the mouth of
Blacksnake Creek on the Missouri
River, 1848, St. Joseph. This is how
Kurz planned to finish his sketches
but apparently never did, with the
exception of this and another one.
Sketch from photographic negative
of the drawing by Rudolph F. Kurz;
courtesy of the St. Joseph Museum

Iowa Indian ready for travel, 1848.
Sketch made from photographic
negative of the drawing by Rudolph F. Kurz; courtesy of the
St. Joseph Museum

Native Americans

Indian man in buckskin. Note method of carrying knife. Sketch made from photographic negative of the drawing by Rudolph F. Kurz; courtesy of the St. Joseph Museum

Iowa Indians on hill, looking down at the young city of St. Joseph, March 9, 1849. Note the court house on top of the hill. Sketch made from photographic negative of the drawing by Rudolph F. Kurz; courtesy of the St. Joseph Museum

Rudolph F. Kurz and his Indian wife, 1850. Sketch made from photographic negative of the drawing by Rudolph F. Kurz; courtesy of the St. Joseph Museum

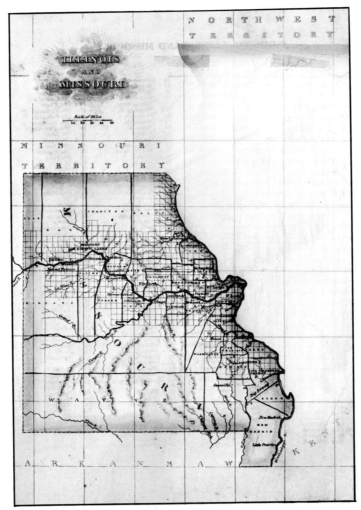

Missouri was admitted as a state to the Union, August 10, 1821. This map of the state of Missouri shows how it was settled in 1825. Photograph courtesy of the St. Joseph Museum

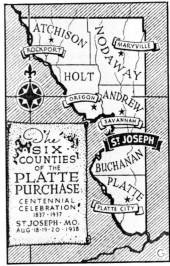

St. Joseph was not always a part of the state of Missouri. It was not until the Platte Purchase of 1837 that the six counties of northwest Missouri—Atchison, Nodaway, Holt, Andrew, Buchanan, and Platte—were added to the state. This is a copy of a poster issued during the 1937 centennial of the purchase. Photograph courtesy of the St. Joseph News-Press

This monument in honor of the Platte Purchase was erected by the Rebecca Rolfe Chapter of the Daughters of American Colonists. Photograph by Don Reynolds; courtesy of the St. Joseph Museum

After the Platte Purchase, the Iowa, Sauk, and Fox Indians were removed by treaty to present Doniphan County, Kansas. With them went Samuel M. and Eliza Irwin, Presbyterian missionaries, who established a log cabin mission and school. A three-story stone and brick building of thirty-two rooms was completed in 1846. Here Indian pupils received elementary schooling and instruction in domestic arts, manual trades, and agriculture. With the organization of Kansas as a territory, the tribes were removed to diminished reserves and the mission was finally closed about 1863 (St. Joseph Museum Graphic).

A portion of the original building of the Highland Presbyterian Mission now houses this state museum approximately thirty miles west of St. Joseph at Highland, Kansas, on K-136. Photograph by Don Reynolds; courtesy of the St. Joseph Museum

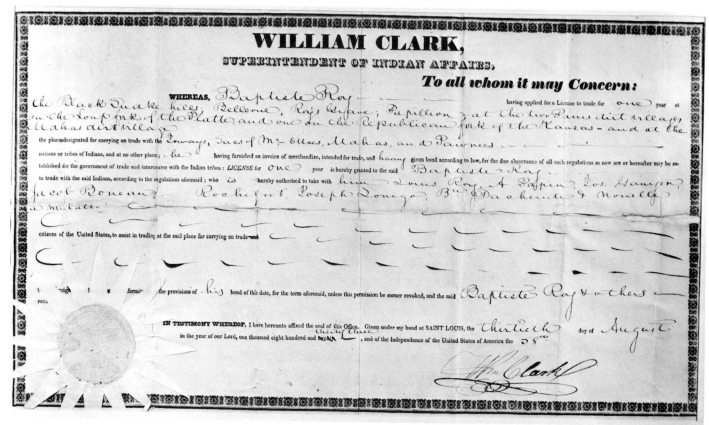

August 13, 1833: William Clark, Superintendent of Indian Affairs, grants Baptiste Roy and others the license to trade for one year with designated Indian tribes at specific locations. Photograph courtesy of the St. Joseph Museum

William P. Richardson, Indian agent. Photograph courtesy of the St. Joseph Museum

The commission of William P. Richardson as agent for all Indian tribes east of the Rocky Mountains and north of New Mexico and Texas was to last from June 1, 1851, for a period of four years. It was personally signed by President Millard Fillmore and Daniel Webster, Secretary of State. The document was given to the St. Joseph Museum by Mrs. Anne Hall Curdy of Kansas City, Richardson's great granddaughter. Photograph courtesy of the St. Joseph Museum

Millard Fillmore

President of the United States of America.
To all who shall see these Presents, Greeting:

Know Ye, That reposing special trust and confidence in the Patriotism, Integrity and Abilities of *William P. Richardson,* I have nominated, and by and with the advice and consent of the Senate, do appoint him to be Agent for the Indian tribes East of the Rocky Mountains, and North of New Mexico and Texas and do authorize and empower him to execute and fulfil the duties of that Office according to Law, and to have and to hold the said Office, with all the powers, privileges and emoluments thereunto legally appertaining, unto him, the said *William P. Richardson,* for the term of four years from and after the thirtieth day of June next.

In Testimony whereof, I have caused these Letters to be made patent and the seal of the United States to be hereunto affixed.

Given under my hand, at the City of Washington, the *twelfth* day of *March,* in the year of our Lord, one thousand eight hundred and *Fifty-One,* and of the Independence of the United States of America, the *Twenty-fifth.*

Millard Fillmore

By the President:

David Webster, Secretary of State.

chapter 2

1826-1848

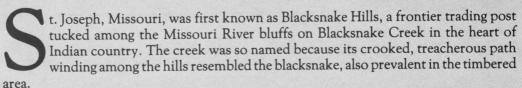

St. Joseph, Missouri, was first known as Blacksnake Hills, a frontier trading post tucked among the Missouri River bluffs on Blacksnake Creek in the heart of Indian country. The creek was so named because its crooked, treacherous path winding among the hills resembled the blacksnake, also prevalent in the timbered area.

St. Joseph was born in 1826. The wild and turbulent Missouri River was its mother. Its father was colorful Joseph Robidoux, a shrewd and friendly French-Canadian fur trader, one of few the Indians liked and trusted. Robidoux was of a St. Louis family who had "practically dug the Missouri River" and had been trading furs along its banks since 1799. Joseph Robidoux was such a fierce competitor the American Fur Company finally bought him out and gave him $1,000 for each year that he would just cool his heels and stay out of the territory.

At the end of three years, the company had another idea. They hired Robidoux at $1,800 per year to operate one of the posts farther down the river. So Robidoux and his party unloaded their keel boats at Roy's Branch, just north of what is now St. Joseph. They didn't like the location, and when spring came they moved down to Blacksnake Creek and built a log cabin post.

Robidoux's small cabin light, made by flickering tallow candles, was the only light from a white habitation glowing in the wilderness within a radius of fifty miles. His trade with the Indians was so lively that he was able to buy the post from the fur company by 1830. At the northeast corner of what is now Second and Jules Street, he built Robidoux's Post, a one and one-half story log structure containing nine rooms and a covered porch. He soon added a grain and saw mill. Robidoux was well known up and down the river, and Indians and fellow traders flocked to the Post, as much to swap tales with the hospitable host as to trade with him.

After the Platte Purchase, settlers began to swarm into the fertile country. The fur trade declined when the gentlemen of New York, London, and Paris ceased wearing beaver hats. But Robidoux, never one to pass up an opportunity, soon realized that even better than fur was the rich soil and timberland he was sitting on. His was a one-man town, and he refused to allow any settler on his claim until he had purchased two quarter-sections of land and had a town platted. He named the town St. Joseph after his patron saint and had it registered in 1843.

The former fur trader-turned-realtor set about carving a town out of the wilderness. Interior lots at $100 and corner sites at $150 went quickly. Robidoux platted more and the town grew—a town as friendly, rollicking and full of vitality as its adventuresome founder.

Joseph Robidoux III, founder of St. Joseph, from a painting by J. V. D. Patch in the St. Joseph Museum. Photograph courtesy of the St. Joseph Museum

Joseph Robidoux, Jr., the son of the
founder of St. Joseph. Also known as
Indian Joe, he died at the age of
eighty-seven on the Iowa Indian
Reservation near White Cloud,
Kansas. Indian Joe's mother, Joseph
Robidoux's first wife, died giving
birth to Indian Joe and his twin
sister, who also died. Joseph Robidoux's second wife bore him six sons
and two daughters. He assured his
wife and children a niche in history
by naming the streets of St. Joseph
after them. Photograph from the
James Treacy Collection; courtesy of
the St. Joseph Museum

Although it could not be proved, this
log cabin was supposedly built in
1826 by the Indians for Joseph
Robidoux and was the first house in
St. Joseph. It stood for years at Krug
Park and was visited by thousands of
persons. Sometime in the 1930s,
park officials decided the cabin was
not actually the Robidoux cabin and
the building was removed. (St. Joseph News–Press). Photograph
courtesy of the Buchanan County
Historical Society

Robidoux's Post where the Black-
snake flowed into the Missouri
River. From a painting by H. E.
Wright; photograph courtesy of the
St. Joseph Museum and Strathmann
Photography

NA-KE-TOM-ME, *wife of Joe Robidoux* MO-NA-KA, *called Indian Joe (1807–1904). Photograph from a print owned by Mrs. Nora Murphy; courtesy of the St. Joseph Museum*

Dr. Silas McDonald was the first physician to practice medicine in Buchanan County, Missouri, coming to the county in 1838. Many of the men of that day wore imported grey woolen capes, a kind of distinguishing mark.

At a meeting of the practicing physicians of St. Joseph and vicinity in 1845, a uniform system of charges was agreed upon. Some of them were:

For a visit within one mile and
   prescription (day) $1.00
For each succeeding mile ... .50
For same service at night, double price
For attendance whole night .. 5.00
For a simple case of midwifery 5.00
For a case of twins 10.00
For extracting teeth .... .50
For amputating fingers and toes, each 5.00
For amputating forearm ... 15.00
For amputating arm 10.00
For amputating leg 20.00
For amputating thigh...... 25.00
For extirpating tumors
.... 2.50 to 10.00
For opening abcesses .... .50
It was also agreed that "no charge will be made for more than two visits in town same day" and "Hereafter, no families will be engaged by the year" (Seward Lilly, History of Buchanan County, Missouri, 1881). Photograph courtesy of the St. Joseph Museum

St. Joseph's first post office was a top hat. When Joseph Robidoux built a log warehouse in the settlement known as Blacksnake Hills, that building also housed the first post office when the federal government opened its postal service there in 1840. When the town was platted and named St. Joseph in 1843, Captain Frederick Smith became the town's first postmaster. Mail from neighboring points was brought by pony and stage riders and left at the post office. Postage was twenty-five cents, and because of the cost, the extent of the mail was not very large (but neither was the town): Postmaster Smith's old-fashioned top hat could easily hold the day's mail. The postmaster was personally acquainted with every inhabitant of the town, and by walking around at his leisure, he could see most of the citizens who had received mail for the day. If not, he would stop at their homes and deliver the letters from his hat, thus giving free city delivery long before many of the more populous cities had ever heard of it (St. Joseph Museum Graphic). Photograph courtesy of the St. Joseph Museum

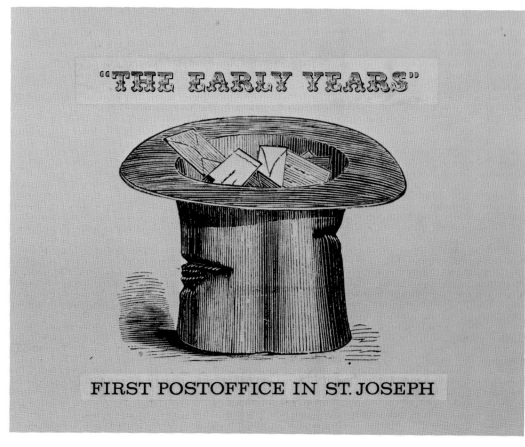

"THE EARLY YEARS"

FIRST POSTOFFICE IN ST. JOSEPH

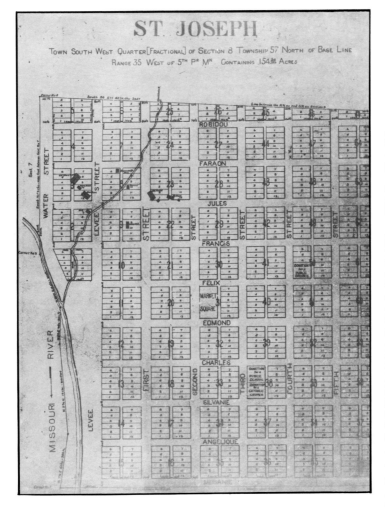

THE FIRST COURT HOUSE, (SPARTA).

Joseph Robidoux employed two surveyors, Simeon Kemper and F. W. Smith, to map out the city and give it a name. Kemper favored "Robidoux" but Smith won with the name "St. Joseph" after Robidoux's patron saint. The town site was registered in St. Louis on July 26, 1843, and August 2, 1843, it was recorded in Buchanan County. The land was the southwest quarter of Section Eight, Township Fifty-seven, Range Thirty-five. It extended from the Missouri River on the west to Sixth Street on the east, and from Robidoux on the north to Messanie Street on the south. The east-west streets were named for members of Robidoux's family—Faraon, Jules, Francis, Felix, Edmond, Charles, Sylvanie, Angelique, and Messanie. Robidoux gave a half-block for a Market Square, a half-block for a public church, and a quarter-block each for a public school and a Catholic Church. Photograph courtesy of the Buchanan County Recorder

This picture is an artist's concept of the first Buchanan County Court House at Sparta. Buchanan County was organized by an act of the legislature on September 10, 1839. The first county court was held in Sparta in the log home of Richard Hill, one of the county judges. The location of the county seat was established at old Sparta on May 25, 1840.

The old town of Sparta was located in Center Township, nine miles south of Blacksnake. At Sparta, a court house was built of logs in 1843 and completed at a cost of $300. "The memorable court house of early times was a house adapted to a variety of purposes, and had a career of great usefulness. School was taught, the gospel preached, and justice dispensed within its substantial walls. Then it served frequently as a resting place for weary travelers, and indeed its doors always swung on easy hinges" (Lilly, History of Buchanan County).

Sparta at the height of its prosperity was only a small town containing three stores, two or three grocery stores, a court house, and a jail. It had a population of about fifteen families. The little town no longer exists but was located on what is now Twenty-Second Street, known as Sparta Road, now Highway 71 (St. Joseph Museum Graphic). Photograph courtesy of the St. Joseph Museum

1826-1848

The old Sparta Cemetery, about 1965. The graveyard was started in 1842, and the first person to be buried in it was a man named Whittle, an overbearing, vindictive ruffian and a terror to the community where he lived. He was killed in 1842 by one Gillett, a peaceable and quiet citizen.

Gillett happened to come into Sparta one day riding a horse when Whittle, who was sitting in front of the dry-goods store, got up, went to Gillett's horse, cut off his tail, and threw it into Gillett's face. Gillett borrowed a pistol from one of the citizens and shot Whittle, who fell in the street, while pursuing Gillett, after he had been shot. The demise of Whittle was the occasion of great rejoicing among his acquaintances. Gillett left the country and was never seen afterward (Lilly, History of Buchanan County). Photograph courtesy of the St. Joseph Museum

When the people of St. Joseph voted to move the county seat to St. Joseph, this two-story brick courthouse was erected at Fourth and Fifth, Jules and Faraon. It was built in 1846 and condemned as unsafe in 1871. The building was razed, and government officials had to have temporary quarters until the present building was constructed. They moved to various places, at one time to a Catholic church on Fifth Street. Photograph courtesy of the St. Joseph News-Press

This photo of William Ridenbaugh is copied from an oil painting presented to the St. Joseph Museum by Edna R. Guernsey. Ridenbaugh came to St. Joseph in 1845 with the equipment for a printing office. He had rescued this equipment from the Missouri River at Independence, where an anti-Mormon mob had thrown it into the river. It had been used by Mormons in printing their paper, the Star of the West. With this press, Ridenbaugh established the St. Joseph Gazette as a weekly newspaper, the first number of which appeared April 25, 1845. This he sold in 1854, but in 1868, he repurchased it and continued as one of its publishers until 1872.(Coy, St. Joseph Museum Graphic). After several ownership changes, the Gazette was purchased by the St. Joseph News-Press in 1928. Today both newspapers are published by The News-Press and Gazette Company. Photograph by Don Reynolds; courtesy of the St. Joseph Museum

26

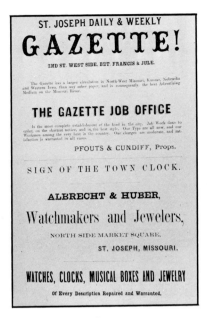

This advertisement for the St. Joseph Daily and Weekly Gazette was taken from a city directory (1859-60). The issue of Friday, April 7, 1848, carried an announcement that Perry, Perry, and Young wanted to purchase any quantity of Hemp, Bacon, Lard, Bee's-Wax, Tallow, and Hides. R. B. Mitchell, Indian Sub Agent, advertised that three stray horses had been taken up in the Indian country and that the owners could secure them by calling him. The Assistant Quartermaster of the U.S. Army at Fort Leavenworth announced that he would receive offers of "up to 1000 yoke of good, well broke, work oxen between the ages of 5 and 9 years" (St. Joseph Museum Graphic). Photograph courtesy of the St. Joseph Museum

Robidoux Row, built by Joseph Robidoux about 1850, is said to be the first apartment house west of the Mississippi River. These apartments were rented free many times to transients whom Robidoux thought would be good citizens. They could stay until financially able to care for themselves. The building still stands. After Robidoux retired from business, he lived in his apartment in Robidoux Row. Sometime during the night, May 28, 1868, he died. He was thought to have choked to death on a cove oyster. (St. Joseph Museum Graphic). Photograph by Don Reynolds; courtesy of the St. Joseph Museum

A back view of Robidoux Row, 1970, before restoration. Photograph by Don Reynolds; courtesy of the St. Joseph Museum

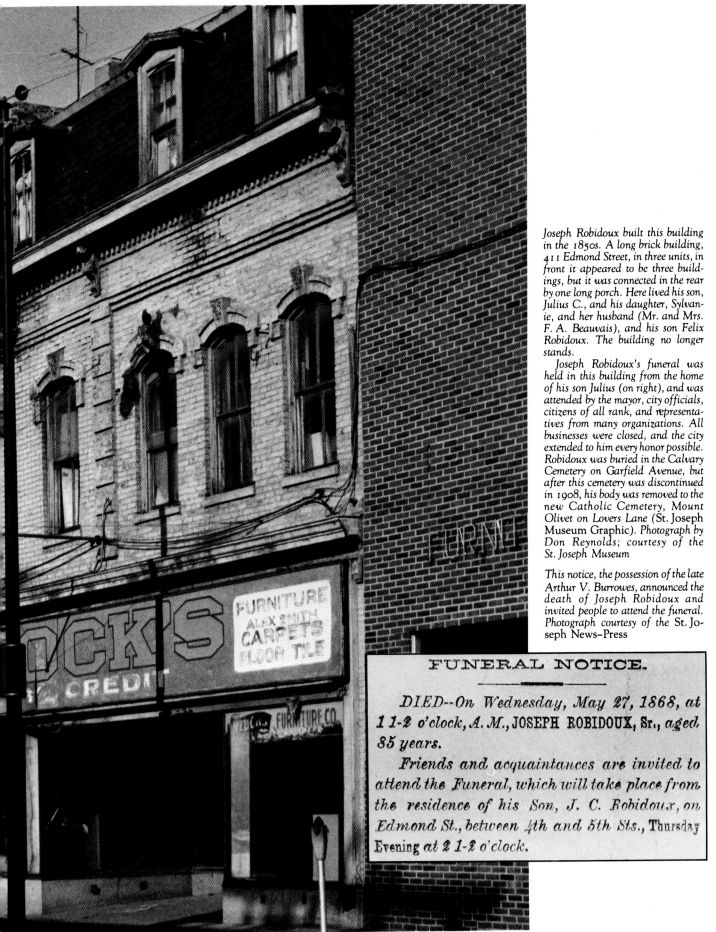

Joseph Robidoux built this building in the 1850s. A long brick building, 411 Edmond Street, in three units, in front it appeared to be three buildings, but it was connected in the rear by one long porch. Here lived his son, Julius C., and his daughter, Sylvanie, and her husband (Mr. and Mrs. F. A. Beauvais), and his son Felix Robidoux. The building no longer stands.

Joseph Robidoux's funeral was held in this building from the home of his son Julius (on right), and was attended by the mayor, city officials, citizens of all rank, and representatives from many organizations. All businesses were closed, and the city extended to him every honor possible. Robidoux was buried in the Calvary Cemetery on Garfield Avenue, but after this cemetery was discontinued in 1908, his body was removed to the new Catholic Cemetery, Mount Olivet on Lovers Lane (St. Joseph Museum Graphic). Photograph by Don Reynolds; courtesy of the St. Joseph Museum

This notice, the possession of the late Arthur V. Burrowes, announced the death of Joseph Robidoux and invited people to attend the funeral. Photograph courtesy of the St. Joseph News–Press

FUNERAL NOTICE.

DIED--On Wednesday, May 27, 1868, at 1 1-2 o'clock, A. M., JOSEPH ROBIDOUX, Sr., aged 85 years.

Friends and acquaintances are invited to attend the Funeral, which will take place from the residence of his Son, J. C. Robidoux, on Edmond St., between 4th and 5th Sts., Thursday Evening at 2 1-2 o'clock.

This etching was purchased by Anne Carter Stauber of St. Louis from a collector and presented to the St. Joseph Historical Society in 1958. Bartlett Boder (St. Joseph Museum Graphic) states that the etching was probably done in 1849 and shows a sidewheel river steamboat passing the Missouri River bluffs just above St. Joseph. He states that the three houses shown were probably on the forward slope of Prospect Hill, a part of the range then known as Blacksnake Hills. In the foreground on the west side of the river, now Kansas, can be seen an Indian teepee and near it the figure of an Indian with bow and arrow shooting at some flying ducks or geese. Hidden by the large trees in the foreground at left is the hilltop site of present-day Wyeth Park.

"Sidewheel steamboats were replaced by stern-wheel boats about Civil War times. What especially fixes the date of this boat are the two steam exhaust pipes to the rear of the smokestacks" (Boder, St. Joseph Museum Graphic). Boder determined that the name of the sidewheel boat was the Robert Campbell Number One. Photograph courtesy of the St. Joseph Museum

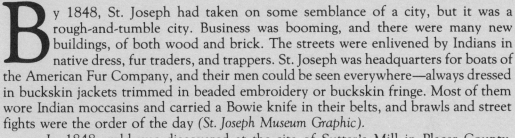

By 1848, St. Joseph had taken on some semblance of a city, but it was a rough-and-tumble city. Business was booming, and there were many new buildings, of both wood and brick. The streets were enlivened by Indians in native dress, fur traders, and trappers. St. Joseph was headquarters for boats of the American Fur Company, and their men could be seen everywhere—always dressed in buckskin jackets trimmed in beaded embroidery or buckskin fringe. Most of them wore Indian moccasins and carried a Bowie knife in their belts, and brawls and street fights were the order of the day (*St. Joseph Museum Graphic*).

In 1848, gold was discovered at the site of Sutter's Mill in Placer County, California. By the spring of 1849, thousands of emigrants were camped around St. Joseph awaiting the overland crossing by wagon train. Some adventuresome inhabitants of the city joined the treks to California to seek the elusive gold, but the more sagacious ones realized there was a gold mine right here in St. Joseph. Merchants, craftsmen, saddle and harness makers, hemp growers, gunsmiths, and pork packers began supplying the gold-seekers at handsome profits. Some of St. Joseph's private fortunes date from that time.

The population of St. Joseph more than doubled in the 1850s. The traffic was largely by steamboat. There was a regular line of sidewheelers between St. Louis and St. Joseph. On each trip several hundred travelers were carried. The cabin fare was from ten to fifteen dollars, including meals.

Steamboat after steamboat stopped at St. Joseph and unloaded passengers, mules, horses, cattle, wagons, and all types of commodities. Along both sides of the river bank, tents could be seen for miles around. Because prices in St. Joseph went up by leaps and bounds, many emigrants had to give up going any farther.

St. Joseph became the second largest city in Missouri, and a wealthy one. In addition to the capitalists who supplied goods and services, overland freighters such as Ben Holladay, Butterfield, Hockaday, and Russell, Majors and Waddell contributed to the city's wealth. Fortunes were made by the steamboat masters. However, the lonesome whistle of the steamboat coming around the bend soon gave way to the shrill neigh of the iron horse. The first train arrived in St. Joseph in 1859, making the city the most western railroad town and sounding the approaching end of river traffic.

Amusements in those days were homespun. The St. Joseph Thespian Society made up of local talent presented stage plays and theatricals. There were also lectures and the wonders of magic lantern shows. The first circus was that of Howes and Mabie in 1846, and for many years St. Joseph was known as a good circus town. (*St. Joseph Museum Graphic*).

In the spring of 1849, thousands of men, women, and children began coming to St. Joseph to outfit for the journey to the California gold fields. It was necessary to wait here until the snows melted in the western country, and by May it was estimated that 20,000 persons were encamped in this vicinity. Another 30,000 were enroute to California by sea.

The Wyeth Hardware and Manufacturing Company was started in 1859 when William M. Wyeth opened a hardware store in St. Joseph to help outfit the wagon trains. The Tootle brothers—Milton, Thomas and Joseph—started in the general mercantile business in 1849

A German artist, Hermann Meyer, sat on the Missouri River bluff near the present St. Joseph Museum and sketched a panoramic view of young St. Joseph, about 1850. The St. Joseph Museum's former Chief Artist, Harry E. Wright, made this faithful reproduction from the early drawing.

The court house, replaced with the present structure, dominates the scene at the upper right, and a steamboat is shown on the Missouri River at the middle left. Missouri

and became prosperous supplying the emigrants bound across the plains to California. Two of the brothers later entered the banking profession. In 1844, Israel Landis opened a Saddle and Harness Shop in St. Joseph, and the enormous traffic of the California gold-seekers brought him prosperity; he later became active in real estate dealing. Outfitting the land expeditions became big business, and the foundations for several St. Joseph firms today may be traced directly to that exciting year when the village of St. Joseph became a city (St. Joseph News-Press). Photograph taken from an old print; courtesy of the St. Joseph News-Press

River bluffs are shown in the upper center. The building with the square tower is St. Joseph's Catholic Church, which stood at Fifth and Felix, to the south of the court house. Most of the buildings in the town were clustered in the flat land adjacent to the river. The view was from the high ground in the vicinity of South Thirteenth Street, south of Messanie Street (St. Joseph Museum Graphic). Photograph courtesy of the St. Joseph Museum

The advertisement from th
St. Joseph directory extols th
advantages of the packet line o
boats which served this area in thos
days. Photograph courtesy of th
St. Joseph Museum

Captain Thomas H. Brierly, whose
country home still stands a few miles
east of St. Joseph, was the operator of
a fleet of luxury steamboats which
plied between St. Louis and St. Joseph (Boder, St. Joseph Museum
Graphic). From a circa-1850 photograph owned by Dr. E. B. Trail;
courtesy of the St. Joseph Museum

The Thomas H. Brierly home, east of
St. Joseph and north of San Antonio,
was built in 1845 with bricks made
by slave labor on the 402-acre farm.
The slave cabins behind the house no
longer exist. It is fifty feet square,
containing eight large rooms with a
large central hall from the ground
floor to the roof, and a floating
stairway to the roof on which parties
were once held (Boder, St. Joseph
Museum Graphic). It is now
vacant and in need of repair.
Photograph by Don Reynolds; courtesy of the St. Joseph Museum

HANNIBAL AND ST. JOSEPH
R. R. PACKET LINE.
THE SPLENDID SIDE-WHEEL STEAMERS,

HESPERIAN, OMAHA,
Capt. KERCHEVAL. Capt. SALTMARSH

EMILIE, Captain La Barge.
LEAVE ST. JOE. TRI-WEEKLY,
DURING NAVIGATION, FOR
BROWNSVILLE, NEBRASKA C'Y, OMAHA, COUNCIL BLUFFS

BLACK HAWK, DESMOINES,
Capt. HAIGHT. Capt. CALVERT.
LEAVE ATCHISON DAILY
On the Arrival of the Cars from St. Joseph, for

This is one of the St. Joseph river packets of the 1850s taken from an advertisement in the 1860 city directory. In appearance it resembles Captain Thomas H. Brierly's famous steamboat, the Polar Star of 1853, which had made a record-breaking trip of two days and twenty hours from St. Louis to St. Joseph.

"As a floating palace, she was proclaimed by many the finest steamboat on any western river. She could seat more than 100 persons, with 10 persons at a table, and carried more than 300 passengers. They were attended by colored waiters clad in tailored evening clothes, wearing white gloves decorated with stars on the gauntlets.... Huge crystal chandeliers hung in the dining saloon which shed the light of many whale oil lamps. The walls of finest wood were painted white and elaborately carved and decorated in gilt.... She had a piano and stringed orchestra, and sometimes a band. After the tables were cleared away at night, the Virginia reel began with a heady noise, stirring to those occupying adjacent bridal chambers which were 'perfect gems of elegance and luxury'" (St. Joseph Museum Graphic). The Polar Star accidently burned near St. Louis in 1859. Photograph courtesy of the St. Joseph Museum and Strathmann Photography

According to Lilly (History of Buchanan County), the Edgar House was built in 1850 on the corner of Francis and Main Streets. It was afterwards long known as the Planter's House. It was at one time the property of John Abell, who kept a hotel in it for a year. United Paper and Office Supply Company is now housed in the building. Photograph courtesy of the St. Joseph Museum

This is the Beauvais House, Second and Michel streets, built by Joseph Robidoux for his daughter in 1850. In 1853, four women of the Society of the Sacred Heart came up from St. Louis on the steamboat Polar Star in order to establish a community of their society in St. Joseph. The four religious first occupied the Beauvais House, and by 1856, the foundation of the permanent St. Joseph convent was laid. The St. Joseph Historic Homes Foundation was formed in 1952 to restore the Beauvais home and the property was bought with donations, but before the work could be done, the house was gutted by fire and had to be razed. Photograph courtesy of the St. Joseph Museum

This is St. Joseph's first Market House and City Hall. When Joseph Robidoux platted St. Joseph, he dedicated one-half block, bounded by Second Street, Francis, and Edmond for a Market House. In 1853, the first Market House was built. It was a brick structure, about fifty by fifty feet. The lower floor was occupied as a market, and all vendors of fresh meat were compelled to locate within. The upper floor at the south end was occupied by city officials (Rutt, History of Buchanan County). Photograph from Rutt, History of Buchanan County

John Corby, an early-day settler and financier in St. Joseph, built Corby's Mill on the 102 River east of St. Joseph in 1852. The shrinking of the 102 River, the advent of steam power, as well as damage from a tornado, doomed the mill, which was razed a number of years ago. It is said the river was named "102" because it is 102 miles long. Photograph from the Max Habecker album; courtesy of the St. Joseph Museum

Governor Robert M. Stewart was the first of the three Missouri governors that St. Joseph provided. He was elected governor on the Democratic ticket in 1857, at which time he was serving the St. Joseph district as state senator, having been elected to the office in 1846. The credit for the building of the Hannibal & St. Joseph Railroad belongs mostly to Governor Stewart, who introduced a bill and secured its passage incorporating the railroad. He is known as Missouri's most eccentric governor. Once, when in his cups in the early hours of the morning, he rode his horse right into the great dining room of the governor's mansion and fed the horse oats from a bowl on the buffet. Governor Stewart died in 1871 (St. Joseph Museum Graphic). Photograph courtesy of the St. Joseph Museum

The Convent of the Sacred Heart building and grounds. The center of the building of the Convent of the Sacred Heart, Twelfth and Messanie, was completed in 1857. The north wing was added in 1884, the south wing in 1890. The records of the convent contain no mention of a stove until 1860. Fireplaces were used for cooking and heating, and a deep well in the back furnished water. Until 1916, cows were kept and vegetable gardens were operated principally by the lay sisters. Sometimes beggars did a little work in return for a meal.

Girls and young women of high school age were taught the things the young Frenchwomen founders of the Society trusted: gentility, courtesy, modesty, and respect for elders. French was taught, for in those days, the girl who couldn't utter a few polite French phrases was not felt to be qualified for aristocratic living. Sewing was also taught and domestic arts to fit the girl pupils to be good wives and mothers (St. Joseph Museum Graphic). Operation of the Convent by the Sacred Heart Society ceased in 1960, and the building became a Catholic high school for girls, named Bishop LeBlond. A new Bishop LeBlond High School, Thirty-Sixth and Frederick, was built in 1961. The old Convent building was razed and apartments built on the site (St. Joseph Museum Graphic). Photograph courtesy of the St. Joseph News-Press

According to Coy (St. Joseph Museum Graphic), the Patee House, Twelfth and Penn streets, was built in 1856-58 by John Patee at a cost of $130,000, the largest and finest hotel west of the Mississippi. It featured 110 guest rooms, winding stairs, and luxurious red Brussels carpets throughout.

Patee House served as a hotel three times, a college twice, and a shirt factory for eighty years. Since 1965, it has been a museum of Western history, owned and operated by the Pony Express Historical Association, Incorporated. It is listed as a Registered National Historical Landmark for its role as headquarters for the Pony Express. Russell, Majors, and Waddell had their offices in this building when they started the Pony Express.

The Hannibal & St. Joseph Railroad's office was in Patee House. Today a restored railroad office and the last Hannibal steam locomotive are displayed there. During the Civil War, the U.S. Provost Marshal's office and the Union army recruiting office were in Patee House. Troops camped on the grounds south of the building.

Patee House was called World's Hotel when Jesse James, who had been a frequent visitor, was killed a block away in 1882. His widow was interviewed by the sheriff at the hotel the next morning. Photograph courtesy of the St. Joseph Museum

St. Joseph Commercial College (Christian Brothers). In 1858, Father James Powers, a pioneer priest, erected a three-story building at Thirteenth and Henry streets and placed it in charge of Christian Brothers. The school was discontinued during the Civil War, and the building was used as barracks by Federal soldiers. The school was reopened in 1867 (Rutt, History of Buchanan County). It was later replaced by a new high school at Union and Noyes Boulevard (St. Joseph News-Press). Photograph from Rutt, History of Buchanan County

According to Rutt (History of Buchanan County), St. Joseph's first City Hospital (to care for charity patients) was on a high bluff on West Robidoux Street. Built of brick, the forty-foot-square building was two stories high and was acquired in 1861. A one-story brick building was erected in 1878. In 1880, an addition was made. In 1880-91, water and lighting were added. This building served as a hospital until 1902, when it was converted into a pest house during an epidemic of smallpox. The city then made a contract with the St. Joseph's Hospital for the maintenance of charity patients. Photograph from Rutt, History of Buchanan County

Built in 1859, the Buchanan County Jail was described by Chris Rutt (History of Buchanan County) as "a house within a house. The inner structure was of brick and cement. The cells only received ventilation through the bars of the doors. The cells were heated by small wood-burning box stoves. There were no sanitary arrangements. Quarters for the female prisoners were in the upper tier of cells." Many people were executed in the jail yard. Hanging was the method of execution. History books report each of the hangings, name of the prisoner, reason he was executed, and events that led to the execution (St. Joseph News-Press). Photograph from Rutt, History of Buchanan County

The Buchanan County Farm was located about two miles northeast of St. Joseph near the Savannah Road. It was a large farm having modern buildings and belonged to the county. The buildings were used to house old men and women who had no means of a livelihood. The main building was badly crowded (Nellie Utz, History of the Growth and Development of St. Joseph). Photograph from Rutt, History of Buchanan County

1848-1860

The building which now houses the Missouri Valley Trust Company, Fourth and Felix, was erected in 1859 for the St. Joseph Branch of the Bank of the State of Missouri on ground purchased from the Robidoux family. The Missouri Supreme Court once met upstairs. Also, Brigham Young did business with the bank while leading a group of Mormons to Utah. It is the oldest building west of the Mississippi River continuously occupied by banking houses. The Missouri Valley Trust Company has occupied the building since 1900 and formerly operated a bank there. It is registered in the National Register of Historic Places (St. Joseph Museum Graphic). Photograph by James Enyeart; collection of Albrecht Art Museum

The interior of the Missouri Valley Trust Company, restored by the owner, Mary Boder, looks much the same as it did when built almost 120 years ago. Pony Express riders, ox-wagon freighters, and stagecoach passengers all warmed themselves at the fireplace before venturing across the great plains. Photograph by Don Reynolds; courtesy of the St. Joseph Museum

Bartlett Boder (St. Joseph Museum Graphic) explains that this five-dollar bank note of 1859 circulated as money, as do the bank notes of the Bank of England. It was issued on May 5, 1859, and was signed by Milton Tootle, President of the Western Bank of Missouri and B. M. (Bela M.) Hughes, cashier of the bank. The Western Bank of Missouri was situated on the northwest corner of Second and Francis streets. The bank note is now classified as an Old Undated Bank Bill and has no value as money, but it is quite valuable as a collector's item. Photograph courtesy of the St. Joseph Museum

The Isaac Miller Home, 3003 Ashland Avenue, was built in 1859. The original grant of land to Isaac Miller was signed by President Polk, and the house has never been out of the Miller family ownership. The family came from Virginia by riverboat and wagon. Bricks were burnt and the home, a twelve-room structure, was built. All the iron work and some of the furniture was sent from St. Louis by riverboat. Photograph by James Enyeart; collection of Albrecht Art Museum

According to Coy (St. Joseph Museum Graphic), this 1871 photo shows the office building of Frederick W. Smith and Son, built in 1859 or 1860. The building faced south on Edmond Street on the corner of the alley east of Sixth Street, Lot One and Two, Block Five, Smith's addition. Major F. W. Smith stands at the left of the picture and F. W. Smith, Jr., is at the right. F. W. Smith, Jr., accidentally shot himself in the knee while standing in front of the door August 22, 1873. He was carried upstairs to the back room, where he died several hours after the accident. Photograph courtesy of the St. Joseph Museum

This is a picture of the old Pioneer Hotel at the southwest corner of Third and Jules, with view to the northwest. Built in the 1860s, it first housed the Bacon Hotel, then the Woodland and Jesse James hotels, before becoming the Pioneer. The building was demolished in 1972 to make a parking lot for the Wyeth Company, Second and Jules. Photograph by Don Reynolds; courtesy of the St. Joseph Museum Collection

As seen by this ad in a St. Joseph City Directory, F. W. Smith was a realtor one door below Edmond. In the latter part of the 1850s, the St. Joseph Thespian Society met at an improvised show house on the second floor of Smith's Hall on Edmond Street. A stage was built and various members of the cast took a hand in painting the scenery. The stage was lighted with small, old-fashioned kerosene lamps, but when they were backed up with new tin reflectors, the stage was a veritable "blaze of glory." And they cleverly devised their own spotlights: when they wanted to stage a tableau, "Rock of Ages," as the curtain went up, a member in the wings ignited a pan of chemicals which burned slowly and cast a beautiful white light. When presenting another tableau, showing the American Indians welcoming Columbus, one of the members discovered that he could make a red

light glow by the addition of a simple chemical. Soon they had formulas for all the lights of the primary colors. They worked well, but all the windows had to be opened for a few minutes after each tableau to let out the almost suffocating strong gas.

The Thespian Society flourished. Some of the plays were: Luke, the Laborer, Pizarro, The Old Blind Man, The Loan of a Lover, and many farce comedies. In 1858, the Thespians were made glad by some real actors from St. Louis who presented Hamlet. The songs of the day rendered by the soloists were "Comin' Through the Rye," "Flow Gently, Sweet Afton," "The Mocking Bird," and "Lilly Dale." Popular dances were the Highland Fling and the Sailor's Hornpipe. The coming of more pretentious show houses soon took the place of Smith's Hall (St. Joseph News–Press).

This advertisement appeared in the St. Joseph city directory of 1860. The Hannibal & St. Joseph Railroad was completed February 13, 1859, and the next day the first passenger train left St. Joseph for the East. On February 22, a special train arrived in St. Joseph bearing a group of officials from St. Louis and Chicago. The next morning, militia in full uniform marched to the martial strains of several brass bands. Prairie schooners, followed by hundreds of citizens, paraded to the mouth of Blacksnake Creek. There, on the spot where he had established his trading post over thirty years before,

stood the venerable, aging Joseph Robidoux. The visitors produced three jugs of water and solemnly performed the ceremony of "the marriage of the waters." They poured water from the Mississippi River, the Atlantic Ocean, and Lake Michigan to mingle with the muddy Missouri—a symbol of the iron tracks that connect the great waters.

The trains ran regularly. St. Joseph was now the western terminal for all railroads in the United States. (Faubion, Tales of Old "St. Joe"). Photograph courtesy of the St. Joseph Museum

NURSING MOTHERS CONVALESCENTS

AND

DELICATE

CHILDREN

Need the Nutritious Combination of Malt and Hops contained in Goetz
To be obtained of all druggists. Do not accept a substitute.

"Pepsotonic"

M. K. GOETZ BREWING COMPANY

ST. JOSEPH, MISSOURI

Try...
Goetz "Pepsotonic"
...of
Malt and Hops
To be Obtained of all Druggists
Telephone 654

BREWERS
BOTTLERS AND
MALSTERS

This is how the first Goetz Brewery looked when it opened in 1859 at Sixth and Albemarle streets. The Goetz family has been benefactors for the St. Joseph Museum and the Pony Express Stables Museum. Photograph courtesy of the St. Joseph Museum

Advertisement by the M. K. Goetz Brewing Company. Photograph from St. Joseph, Missouri, a souvenir booklet by the United Commercial Travelers of America

chapter 4

The Pony Express

Practically the whole western world was watching Missouri April 3, 1860. That day a stripped-down, one-coach train of the Hannibal & St. Joseph Railroad was rushing across the state at full speed, bearing the eastern mail to be delivered to the first Pony Express rider at St. Joseph. At about six o'clock, the little "Boo Hoo" locomotive, Missouri, was heard approaching town, its wailing whistle giving warning to clear the tracks and be prepared. A cannon boomed from in front of Patee House, and cheers reached the sky from a thousand throats. The mail was quickly transferred to the mochila of the rider, and the mayor gave the sorrel pony a slap on the rump. Horse and rider dashed to the ferry which carried them across the Missouri River. They mounted the slippery bank and disappeared into the gloom. Nearly 2,000 miles away, another rider had set his face to the East and was hurrying toward the approaching messenger beginning his dangerous journey (*St. Joseph Museum Graphic*).

Ten days later, exactly on time, a Pony Express rider galloped into Sacramento. The first Pony Express American Mail system had begun. Organized by Russell, Majors, and Waddell from St. Joseph to Sacramento, California, the Pony Express established a direct line of communication between the East and the West. A route was mapped out; 80 to 100 riders (few over eighteen years of age, mostly orphans) and 400 to 500 horses were engaged.

The Pony Express operated for eighteen or nineteen months. At the end of that time its usefulness was completed, for a telegraph line had been installed from Omaha to Sacramento.

St. Joseph's part in the romantic episode shines through history as a pioneering accomplishment. However, due to the turmoil of the Civil War, during which time records and newspapers were destroyed and burned, and the sheer urgency of the fast pace at which history was being pounded out, few authentic records of this colorful period in St. Joseph's history can be found. So the complete, unchallenged chapter will probably never be written.

The Pony Express meets the Hannibal & St. Joseph train at the railroad station near Eighth and Olive streets. In the background is one of the Concord stagecoaches of the Central Overland California and Pike's Peak Express Company. These stagecoaches also called at the Patee House before starting across the plains (Boder, St. Joseph Museum Graphic). It is now believed that mail went from train to post office to be stamped and picked up there by the rider coming from the stables. Photograph from an artist's concept; courtesy of the St. Joseph Museum

The Missouri was the locomotive which made the dash across the state of Missouri, April 3, 1860, drawing the one-coach train bearing the Pony Express mail from the east to St. Joseph, to be carried on the backs of horses to California. She was a Mason-type engine built expressly for the Hannibal & St. Joseph Railroad in 1858. The Missouri also hauled the first postal mail car used in the United States in July 1862 between Hannibal and St. Joseph, according to Boder (St. Joseph Museum Graphic).

"Locomotives on the Hannibal & St. Joseph often bore names of famous people, cities, towns, and counties through which the trains passed. The huge smokestacks reminded men of the hoop skirts worn by women, only up-side-down. This then made them think of the name of a famous concert singer who wore hoop skirts. So the smokestacks were named after the singers" (Boder, St. Joseph Museum Graphic). Photograph courtesy of the St. Joseph Museum

The ferryboat the Denver, which at 7:30 P.M. on April 3, 1860, is said to have carried the bay mare and the first pony rider out of St. Joseph and across the Missouri River into Kansas territory at Elwood (Boder, St. Joseph Museum Graphic). Photograph courtesy of the St. Joseph Museum

Pony Express map by Harry E. Wright on display in the Pony Express Stables Museum. Research for the map was done by Bartlett Boder, Don Reynolds, and Roy E. Coy. Photograph courtesy of the St. Joseph Museum

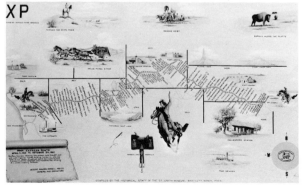

Benton Clark's original painting portrays Pony Express rider Richard Cleve, who made a 160-mile ride in 1861 through a raging blizzard, deep snow, and biting cold (St. Joseph Museum Graphic). Photograph courtesy of the St. Joseph Museum

Departure of the first Pony Express mail from the Pike's Peak Pony Express Stables on Penn Street, April 3, 1860, showing the present day Pony Express Museum in the background.

The St. Joseph Weekly Free Democrat of April 7, 1860, describes this important occasion: "On last Tuesday evening the pony express of Messrs. Majors, Russell & Company started from this city amid the shouts and cheers of hundreds of persons who had gathered together on the spot from whence it was to depart, to witness the opening of this grand enterprise. All being desirous of preserving a memento of the flying messenger, the little pony was almost robbed of his tail" (Lilly, History of Buchanan County). From an oil painting by Charles Hargems; courtesy of the St. Joseph Museum

The Pony Express

A copy of the St. Joseph Gazette printed on tissue paper was carried to California on the first Pony Express out of St. Joseph. A photostatic copy of that issue was given to the St. Joseph Historical Society by the California State Society. The first mail to California took ten days en route. To perform these services required some 160 relay and home stations and over 400 employees, including station keepers and stock or horse tenders. The relay stations were ten to fifteen miles apart and the only company for some station keepers was "the hot burning sand and a few lizards" (Boder, St. Joseph Museum Graphic). Photograph courtesy of the St. Joseph Museum

Most colorful of the St. Joseph Pony Express riders was Johnny Fry. He was young, handsome, single, and a favorite among the girls of the day. It is said that the Kansas maidens waited along the trail for Johnny Fry to pass and offered him cookies and sweets. However, Johnny was traveling so fast at times it became difficult to hand these tidbits to him, so one unknown young lady invented a cookie with a hole in it, making it easier for Johnny on his fast steed to pick it up. This, so the story goes, was the beginning of the doughnut. Another legend describes the time Johnny was riding at Troy, Kansas, and a young woman on a fresh horse overtook him and tore off a corner of his loose shirt, which she included in a patchwork quilt she was making (Boder, St. Joseph Museum Graphic). Photograph found in the old historical files at the St. Joseph Museum; courtesy of the St. Joseph Museum

This photograph is from an original painting, Changing the Mochila, by Benton Clark. Two minutes were allowed for the mount and mail mochila change, but many of the riders were able to cut the time to fifteen seconds. Photograph courtesy of the St. Joseph Museum

This photograph of four St. Joseph Pony Express riders shows, left to right, standing, William (Billy) Richardson and Johnny Fry; seated are Charlie Cliff and Gus Cliff. The 1860 city directory of St. Joseph shows Johnny Fry as foreman of Fish and Robidoux Livery Stables, Main and Faraon streets, and Richardson is listed as hostler at the same livery stable (St. Joseph Museum Graphic). The Pony Express riders were paid $125 per month. Photograph courtesy of the St. Joseph Museum

This copy of the painting was given to the St. Joseph Museum in 1949 by the History Room at the Wells Fargo Bank in San Francisco. It depicts how San Francisco welcomed the Pony Express the night of April 13-14, 1860. "Sacramento had declared a holiday," writes Bartlett Boder in the St. Joseph Museum Graphic. "Bands were out. Top-hatted dignitaries were out as they had been in St. Joseph....The rider was noisily escorted to the Alta Telegraph office where the Sacramento mail was delivered....With wild cheers the rider, his pony, and the San Francisco mail were escorted aboard the sidewheeler steamboat Antelope....In San Francisco, there was much speech-making at the telegraph office at the corner of Merchant and Montgomery streets with singing and dancing and music by the bands. The fun lasted until near daybreak of April fourteenth. The Pony Express after thirteen years had answered California's great need." Photograph courtesy of the St. Joseph Museum

The Pony Express

This St. Joseph news account gives the time and rates of the Pony Express. Only three or four of the Pony Express riders were known to have been killed by the Indians while they were riding the trail. Even then, the ponies arrived at the next stations with the mail on time. Photograph courtesy of the St. Joseph Museum

CENTRAL OVERLAND CALIFORNIA
AND
PIKE'S PEAK EXPRESS CO.

PONY
EXPRESS!

FROM SAINT JOSEPH, MO.,
TO
SAN FRANCISCO
IN TEN DAYS!

(FIFTEEN DAYS DURING WINTER,)

Passes through, and takes Letters to the following points:
Fort Kearney,
Fort Laramie,
Fort Bridger,
Great Salt Lake City,
Camp Floyd,
Virginia City,
Carson City,
Placerville

and Sacramento City.

CHARGES.

Letters not exceeding ¼ oz.,.................... $2 50
" over ¼ oz. and not exceeding ½ oz. 5 00
and so on, always to be pre-paid.

AGENTS.

J. B. Simpson, New York ; Cobb, Candler & Co., Boston
W. H. Warder, Chicago ; Samuel & Allen, St. Louis ; J. F
Caldwell, Washington City.

St. Joseph Office at Patee House.

Replica of the Pony Express saddle bags (mochila) in the Pony Express Stables Museum. The saddle was especially designed and made by Israel Landis of St. Joseph. It was in two sections so the leather mochila with its four mail pockets (two on each side) could be easily moved from the saddle proper and put without delay on the next relay horse. Photograph courtesy of the St. Joseph Museum

Pony Express rider passing the overland telegraph line builders. "Late in the year 1860, the telegraph had been started on up river from St. Joseph . . . . On October 24, 1861, the last connection was made at Salt Lake City, and a slender strand of wire, the first transcontinental overland telegraph, took over the job of rapid communication between East and West. The Pony Express could now rest. A job well done" (Don Reynolds, St. Joseph Museum Graphic). Painting by William H. Jackson; photograph courtesy of the St. Joseph Museum

52

Pony Express rider Michael Whalen and wife, Susan. The rugged riders on the toughest horse flesh of their time averaged nearly ten miles an hour between stations and rode daylight and dark, through sunshine, rain, or snow. Photograph courtesy of the St. Joseph Museum

On May 3, 1959, the Pony Express Stables Museum—located on the original stable site from which the first rider left St. Joseph on April 3, 1860—was opened as a part of the St. Joseph Museum. In 1959, M. Karl Goetz, then president of the M. K. Goetz Brewing Company, and the brewing company, together contributed funds toward the operation of the Pony Express Stables Museum. Around 1960, after Goetz passed away and the Goetz Brewing Company was no longer a St. Joseph owned operation, support for the Pony Express Stables Museum came entirely from the St. Joseph Museum budget (St. Joseph Museum Graphic). The monument marks the starting place of the Pony Express. Photograph courtesy of the St. Joseph Museum

The Pony Express

This United States Mail Car Number One was the invention of William A. Davis, assistant postmaster in St. Joseph, according to Boder (St. Joseph Museum Graphic). It was first used July 28, 1862, to bring mail from West Quincy, Missouri, to St. Joseph. Because of delays two years before in having mail sorted for the Pony Express, Davis made a drawing of his plan for the mail car and submitted it to Postmaster J. L. Bittinger, who in turn submitted it to Postmaster General Montgomery Blair in Washington, D.C. Two such cars were ordered built at the railroad shops at Hannibal under the supervision of Davis. Though the Pony Express had long ceased to exist when the two cars were put into use, they were needed to protect the mail and the messenger from being shot through windows by guerillas, for the Civil War was on. Photograph courtesy of the St. Joseph Museum

M. Karl Goetz (May 23, 1909-January 16, 1960) was a lifelong resident of St. Joseph. During World War II, he served as chief of the overseas assignment branch of the Army Air Corps Personnel Division, holding the rank of Colonel. He was very active in all phases of the Pony Express and the Pony Express Museum (St. Joseph Museum Graphic). Photograph by Shultz Studio; courtesy of the St. Joseph Museum

This Pony Express Memorial statue graces the Civic Center, Frederick Avenue at Ninth. The marker is a life-sized bronze statue of a Pony Express rider and his mount. The monument was unveiled April 20, 1940, and weighs 7,200 pounds. It was done by the late H. A. MacNeil of New York (St. Joseph Museum Graphic). Photograph by Don Reynolds; courtesy of the St. Joseph Museum

THE PONY EXPRESS
St. Joseph, Missouri

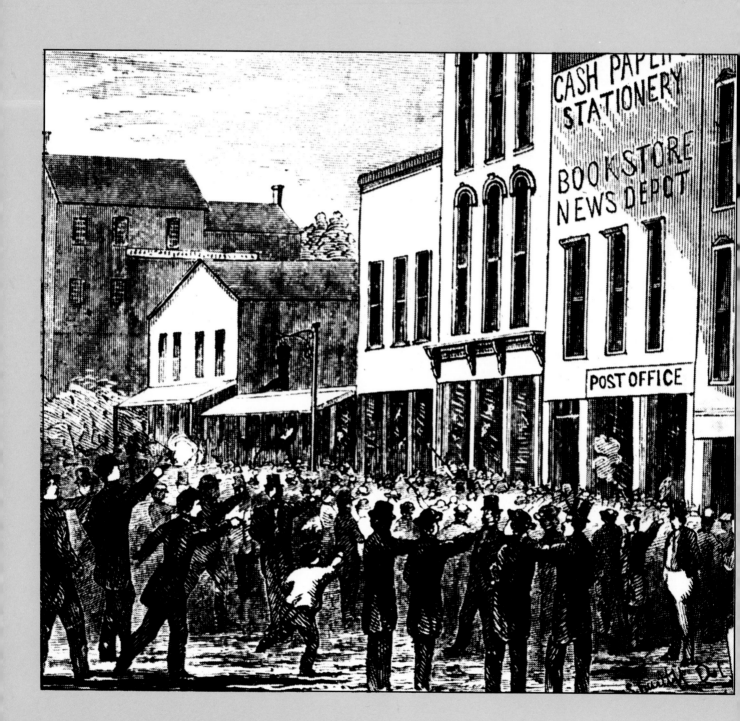

chapter 5

The Civil War

This was the scene in May 1861 which brought Federal troops and martial law to St. Joseph. According to the St. Joseph Museum Graphic, in order to stop provocations, the city council had passed an ordinance forbidding the flying of any flags— either pro-slavery or Northern. A new pro-Union postmaster, John L. Bittinger, hoisted the Stars and Stripes on the post office (then situated on the east side of Second Street north of Francis). A crowd immediately gathered to protest. Former Mayor M. Jeff Thompson came from his office to help calm the crowd. (He later admitted he got carried away and personally led the mob in tearing the flag from the building.) Thompson left St. Joseph the next day to join Confederate troops for the remainder of the Civil War.

The flag was ripped to pieces; the pole was broken off and lowered to the screaming, milling mass of people, who carried it to the bank of the Missouri River where it was cast into the water. As evening drew a curtain of night upon the riotous scene, the mob fury rose to a higher crescendo. Riverfront taverns were looted, and "Old Red Eye and Panther squall" whiskey helped to befuddle, confuse, and lessen control. Stores suffered; looting was widespread. Negro shanties along the waterfront were burned, some occupants escaping with only their lives.

Many historians believe the flag incident had an unfortunate effect on St. Joseph, for the government moved the entire eastern terminus of the proposed Union Pacific Railroad from St. Joseph to Omaha. St. Joseph lost its place as the metropolis of the Missouri River Valley, never to gain it back (St. Joseph Museum Graphic). Photograph courtesy of the St. Joseph Museum

The Civil War was in many respects the sorriest chapter in the colorful history of St. Joseph. The city was a border city in a border state and settled largely by people from Southern states. The presence of more than 2,000 slaves valued at over $1,500,000 explains the strong pro-slavery sentiment by a large portion of the community. But St. Joseph had a railroad to the East and a Pony Express to the West and was quite mercantile minded. Its merchants were making fortunes in the vast Western country. They also welcomed the Northerners who augmented both population and property values. The city tried to maintain a middle-of-the-road attitude and at the same time to keep support of its elected men.

When Lincoln was elected president in 1860, Missouri gave him only 10 percent of the vote. Soon after the election, South Carolina seceded from the union. Within six weeks, six other states seceded. In Missouri, there was great controversy whether the state should secede. Governor Claiborne Jackson declared that no Missouri troops would fight their brother Southerners. When the call came for the Missouri troops to help suppress the Southern rebellion, the town of St. Joseph fractured. Tension was so great that a "little Civil War" was feared. Brother turned against brother; neighbor against neighbor. Feelings ran high; hate was rampant.

After the notorious mob removal of the flag, Mayor Smith, a staunch Union man, seeing no hope of bringing the lawless crowd under control, wired for help to the Federal troops at Fort Leavenworth (*St. Joseph Museum Graphic*).

The next day, the United States Dragoons were sent to St. Joseph to help quell the civil disturbance. From then on, there was a succession of military troops in the city. When the troops moved out, mobs and rioting prevailed. Merchants ferried their stocks to Elwood and concealed them. What was left behind was stolen. Nearly every business was closed down. The city went backward, as other towns did: men were out of work; real estate values slumped; fortunes were swept away.

There was guerilla war. The railroad bridge over the Platte River was destroyed, and a train carrying ninety-four passengers plunged into the stream. Only three were uninjured. The eighteen dead were brought to the depot at Eighth and Olive streets and laid out in an open-air, temporary morgue.

Fewer trains ran. The government commandeered the riverboats. The town's confidence was destroyed, and never again would she be the proud Queen of the River.

The Civil War

M. Jeff Thompson, mayor of St. Joseph 1859-60. In this photo he is Brigadier General. After the flag incident, Thompson left St. Joseph bearing the title of Brigadier General and soon became prominent in his conduct of the war in southeastern Missouri. In keeping with his interest in railroads, one of his first acts was to lead a Confederate raid on the St. Louis and Iron Mountain Railroad when he secured 18,000 pounds of lead for the Southern cause. He was so successful that he was soon known as the "swamp fox," after the swamp regions of Missouri and Arkansas from which he operated. Thompson was captured in August 1863 by the Missouri State Militia at Pocahontas, Arkansas. Captain Reuben Kay was one of Thompson's three cavalry staff who was captured along with him. Thompson was taken first to Gratiot prison in St. Louis and then to Ohio, where he was kept until his release at the end of the war. He returned to St. Joseph in 1876 suffering with "consumption." He died September 2, 1876, at the age of fifty at the Pacific House Hotel, not 200 feet from the scene of the 1861 flag incident. Burial was at Mt. Mora cemetery (St. Joseph Museum Graphic). *Photograph courtesy of the St. Joseph Museum*

This is a photograph of the first "Turnhalle," known as the "Cradle of Liberty," Seventh and Charles streets. The cornerstone of the building was laid March 29, 1860. The "Turn-Vereins," a group of German-Americans, was formed May 23, 1855. When the Civil War broke out, the Turners staunchly avowed loyalty to the Union. Their hall was dubbed the "Cradle of Liberty," and the stars and stripes were boldly flung to the breeze. When the mob that had taken the flag at the post office declared the Turner flag should also be torn from the staff, two Turners went upon the roof in the face of danger, lowered the flag, and brought it safely inside. The second Turner Hall was built on the same site in 1890 (Rutt, *History of Buchanan County*). The Turner Hall was torn down in 1978. *Photograph from Rutt, History of Buchanan County*

Reuben Kay, son of James Kay, well-to-do dry goods merchant of St. Joseph. After his graduation from the Kentucky Military Institute in 1858, he returned to St. Joseph. Reuben, a handsome young man, immediately plunged into the social swim of the city. He attended all the social events, dances, and parties that the bustling city could boast of. He also joined the Jackson Guards, Volunteer Militia of Missouri. The militia held the finest social events of the year. It was the social register of young men. There was not much formal drill but many fancy uniforms, and the annual musters were always a big event for barbeques, dances, and drinking. They made the parades for great events, such as the first train into St. Joseph and the start of the Pony Express.

War came to St. Joseph the spring of 1861 and with it an end of the social whirl people had known. The militia companies disbanded, and young Kay eventually made his way South, most likely on the Underground Railroad. There he joined M. Jeff Thompson, who was recruiting at Martinsburg, in southeast Missouri. Kay fought with the "swamp fox" until the war's end in 1865 (St. Joseph Museum Graphic). Photograph courtesy of the St. Joseph Museum

The Battle of Lexington, September 12-20, 1861. Many St. Joseph men participated in this battle as Confederate soldiers. A regiment to join Price at Lexington was organized from the counties of Buchanan, Nodaway, Atchison, and Andrew in August 1861. These troops were placed under the command of Colonel Green at Lexington and were the special heroes of that fight. Colonel Green, in his report of the battle, attributed the success of the assault upon the Union breastworks to the devices of Major Thornton's men of this regiment, in moving a bale of hemp in front of each man as he cautiously ascended the hill to attack the entrenchments. The bullets did not penetrate the hemp bales, and the cannon balls only bounced them from the ground, the bales falling back in the same position (Lilly, History of Buchanan County). Photograph courtesy of the St. Joseph Museum

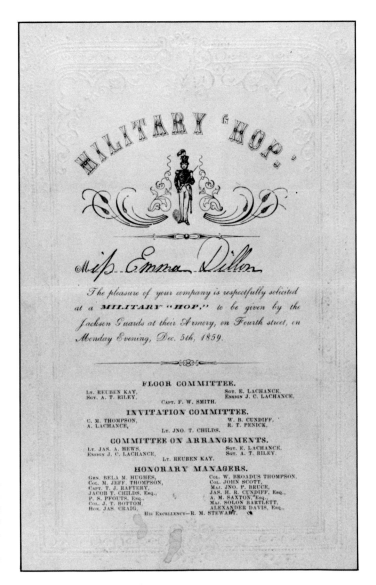

This is a copy of a perfectly preserved invitation to a Military "Hop" given by the Jackson Guards in St. Joseph, December 5, 1859. The company was one of the three militia units in the city at the time and was rated as pro-Southern in its sympathies. The invitation was extended to Miss Emma Dillon; it was presented to the St. Joseph Historical Society by its charter member Daniel J. Patton (St. Joseph Museum Graphic). Photograph courtesy of the St. Joseph Museum

Battle of Wilson's Creek, near Springfield, Missouri, August 10, 1861, between the forces under General Lyon and General McCulloch. In this engagement, General Lyon was killed (Lilly, History of Buchanan County). Besides the militia organizations mustered into service from the county, equally as many went into the army, making fully 4,000 soldiers who did duty for the old flag from St. Joseph and Buchanan County. Photograph courtesy of the St. Joseph Museum

Dug Cut, view to the south, from the bridge, at that time called Paris Avenue. In October 1861, the Sixteenth and the Fifty-Second Illinois Infantry arrived by the Hannibal & St. Joseph Railroad, unloaded at the depot at Eighth Street and proceeded to Prospect Hill where a camp was set up. The Federal forces then raised a breastworks along the edge of the hill. A legend in St. Joseph claims that the same troops dug a road through a hill, also, in order to facilitate the moving of supply wagons (Charles Radcliffe, St. Joseph Museum Graphic). Dug Cut has been widened and is now a part of the West Belt Highway project. Photograph by Don Reynolds; courtesy of the St. Joseph Museum

A bird's-eye view of St. Joseph, 1868. The view is to the southeast, with the Missouri River in the foreground. A steamboat is plying the river, and a Kansas City, St. Joseph & Council Bluffs railroad train is shown at the lower left. At the top of the bluff near the center of the picture are the earthen walls of Union entrenchments built by two regiments of Illinois troops in 1861 to guard St. Joseph and the river.

The men of the regiments conducted themselves as guests, except for one incident. J. H. R. Cundiff, editor of the Gazette, was a pro-Southern man, and he stated his views vocally in his paper. The Union soldiers soon grew tired of this constant tirade of abuse and scorn heaped upon them and the country they had sworn to serve. In January 1862, a delegation went to talk to the fiery editor. They were joined by more soldiers when the word about their destination spread. The editor, brave, but not foolhardy, left town on a fast horse to go South. (He returned a colonel after the war). When the soldiers found the editor had left, they proceeded to destroy the presses and the paper, to carry off the type to be melted down for lead bullets, and to set the building on fire (St. Joseph Museum Graphic). From an original print owned by John P. Beihl; photograph courtesy of the St. Joseph Museum

61

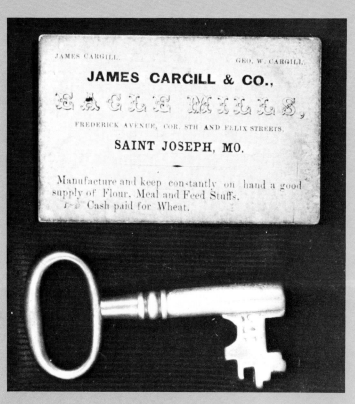

JAMES CARGILL.   GEO. W. CARGILL.

JAMES CARGILL & CO.,

EAGLE MILLS,

FREDERICK AVENUE, COR. 8TH AND FELIX STREETS.

SAINT JOSEPH, MO.

—

Manufacture and keep con-tantly on hand a good supply of Flour, Meal and Feed Stuffs.

☞ Cash paid for Wheat.

This is the brass key to the Cargill flour mill which George Cargill took with him when he fled from St. Joseph. The key is now framed in the residence of John P. Cargill in Kansas City (St. Joseph Museum Graphic). Photograph courtesy of the St. Joseph Museum

In 1860, George W. Cargill and John Colby Cargill operated the family's steam flour mill on Felix between Eighth and Ninth streets. Misfortune overtook the family in the War Between the States. As Southern sympathizers, they suffered the fate of many who gave their allegiance to the cause of the Confederacy. Their farm was looted, their slaves left home, their big flour mill was burned, and they were practically banished. John Cargill was held in jail. George Cargill fled at night on horseback and made his way through the Union lines to Virginia (Boder, St. Joseph Museum Graphic). Photograph courtesy of the St. Joseph Museum

General Odon Guitar was in the third class to graduate from the University of Missouri. General Guitar was promoted to his rank in the Enrolled Missouri Militia by virtue of his gallantry while serving with the Missouri State Militia in central Missouri. He accompanied General Alexander W. Doniphan on that general's famous expedition to Mexico in the War with Mexico in 1846. After leaving St. Joseph, Guitar distinguished himself at the fighting at Boonville, Missouri, October 13, 1863. This photograph is from a painting by J. Sidney Brown (St. Joseph Museum Graphic). Photograph courtesy of the St. Joseph Museum

The Civil War

Colonel Elijah Gates, the one-armed "Fighting Rebel," came to St. Joseph in 1857 and entered the Missouri State Guard in 1861 as a captain. During the Civil War, he was wounded five times; three times captured, twice making his escape; and had three horses shot from under him. He fought in the engagements at Carthage, Dry Wood, Lexington, and Springfield, Missouri. He organized a regiment at Springfield and was commissioned Colonel. Gates fought in the battle at Elk Horn, Arkansas. When charging the breastworks at Franklin, Tennesee, he was shot by a Minie ball in his left arm and his right arm below the elbow: his left arm had to be amputated. Captured by the Federals and ordered north to prison, he escaped from the railroad train in the dark and found his way to a regiment in Mobile. The regiment was overcome in the last battle of the Civil War.

Returning to St. Joseph, Colonel Gates in 1865 started in the livery business on Fourth Street and continued there until he was elected sheriff of Buchanan County in 1871. In 1876, he was elected State Treasurer of Missouri. In 1881, he became a partner in the omnibus line of Price and Gates. He was also a director of the Hannibal & St. Joseph Railroad (St. Joseph Museum Graphic). Photograph courtesy of the St. Joseph Museum

This photograph shows General Odon Guitar inspecting a newly formed unit of the Enrolled Missouri Militia, nicknamed the Pawpaws, in 1863. Although they had not yet been issued muskets, the new recruits wore the Union blue uniforms and drilled with broomsticks. General Guitar, at the extreme right of the picture, is identified by his heavy black beard. G. W. Brown's store and tin shop was on the east side of Second Street north of Francis Street. The three-story building dimly seen at the right was occupied by Bryant's Business College, and just beyond it was the Post Office building from which the flag was lowered by M. Jeff Thompson in 1861.

The name Pawpaws for the Enrolled Missouri Militia came from the saying that it was partly made up of Southern sympathizers who had been hiding out in the pawpaw bushes. By rendering nominal allegiance to the Union, these men performed great service in protecting both Northern and Southern men from marauders (Boder, St. Joseph Museum Graphic). Photograph courtesy of the St. Joseph Museum

As the Civil War fighting moved deeper South, St. Joseph was left in the backwash of war. A huge hospital was established in the Sacred Heart Convent. St. Joseph watched the blue columns of troops leave the town, headed for the swamps on the Yazoo or the rifle pits at Vicksburg, then saw them come back on a steamboat and be carried up the hill to the hospital, from which they would either limp away minus an arm or a leg or be carried out in a pine box while muffled drums beat the dirge. To those who were left behind, it mattered not if the one who had left to fight wore the Blue or the Gray. There was a oneness in the sorrow of a letter telling of a lonely grave at Vicksburg, Corinth, or Iuka. Too often the only epitaph for many was in the family Bible: "John has gone to war—1861" (Radcliffe, St. Joseph Museum Graphic). *Photograph from the Frank Zbierski Collection; courtesy of Strathmann Photography*

St. Joseph in 1861, as seen from the
Kansas side of the Missouri River,
looking toward the southeast, in a
view taken from the Illustrated
London News. The building with
the dome is the court house which
preceded the present structure. The
steamboat St. Louis, is shown at the
middle left. The fact that St. Joseph
is built on the Missouri River bluffs
is very evident. Photograph courtesy
of the St. Joseph Museum

chapter 6

1860-1880

After the Civil War, St. Joseph, like a giant awakening from a hideous nightmare, aroused itself and looked around with unbelieving eyes at the destruction, then, with characteristic frontier spirit, took a deep breath, rolled up its sleeves, and started anew.

The results were almost incredible. By the end of 1871, the local press reported: "Never in any previous period in her history has St. Joseph been favored with as large a wholesale trade as during the past year." As the Missouri River had at first been the lifeblood of St. Joseph, the railroads now were. Throughout the state, the railroads had spread quickly, and St. Joseph, sharing many of them, attracted new industries and was for a time the wholesale drygoods capital of the Midwest. With the resumption of trade, the city's population began to double almost every ten years.

Schools were reopened in 1864, and many new ones were built. The year 1880 showed sixty-seven public school teachers on the payroll here with an average annual salary of $564.

At the close of the decade, the Krugs, Hax Brothers, A. O. Smith, David Pinger, and Connett Brothers were packing pork on a large scale, and at the Union Stock Yards on South Tenth Street there was a lively market in competition with Kansas City.

A new City Hall was built along with many other downtown buildings. New brick streets were spreading out from downtown. With the population mushrooming, the need for city services became apparent. Fire and police forces were organized, telephones were installed, and gas became the main form of street and home lighting.

The Buchanan County Court House was built in 1873-76. The size of the splendid Neo-Classical structure, second largest in the state, indicated expectations of great growth and a spirit of confidence and optimism among the citizens.

As the city's prosperity increased, people found they had more time for aesthetic interests. Milton Tootle, Sr., constructed his spectacular Tootle Opera House on Francis Street so that St. Joseph could enjoy the beauty and glamour of life on the stage.

However, in spite of all the growth and prosperity, citizens had their frustrations. *The Daily News* made its appearance in St. Joseph in 1879. In December a long story described the rising food costs: "Flour has advanced, best grade, $1.50 per barrel and now holds firm at prices $5.50 and $7.50 per barrel....There has been a medium increase in price in potatoes from 55¢ to 60¢ per bushel. Pickles have advanced 10 percent, syrups the same, crackers have risen from 6¢ to 7¢ per pound" (*St. Joseph Museum Graphic*).

Josephine Angelique Robidoux was a student of the Academy of the Sacred Heart early in 1861 when she received Francis P. Corby of Cincinnati, Ohio, in the visitor's room. It was probably then that this gifted granddaughter of Joseph Robidoux, the city's founder, received her proposal of marriage. Corby was a widower, forty-one years of age, and she was eighteen, the daughter of Felix Robidoux. The couple was married in 1861 (St. Joseph Museum Graphic). Photograph courtesy of the St. Joseph Museum

The records of the Superintendent of St. Joseph Schools show that in 1861 the School Board authorized E. B. Neely to conduct a high school in his Academy building at Tenth and Felix streets and to charge one dollar a month tuition. Forty teen-age students, girls and boys, enrolled (Boder, St. Joseph Museum Graphic). The building was removed by urban renewal in the 1970s and was later demolished. Photograph courtesy of the St. Joseph Museum

This photograph of E. B. Neely in 1875 is a part of the Lozo collection at the St. Joseph Public Library. At the time of his death in 1904, Professor Neely had been superintendent of St. Joseph public schools since August 1864. In 1866, he was elected superintendent of schools of Buchanan County. He served three two-year terms. Professor Neely's reputation as an educator gradually became nation-wide, and his opinions on educational matters were often sought from coast to coast. (Boder, St. Joseph Museum Graphic). Photograph courtesy of the St. Joseph Museum

In 1860, William Ridgeway Penick was a senior partner in Penick and Loving, wholesale druggists and booksellers in St. Joseph, and a member of the city council. He introduced an ordinance providing for the creation of a fire department since the citizens of the city had nothing but the Bucket Brigade to protect their homes from fire. It was not until 1864, when Mr. Penick was elected mayor, that the ordinance was passed. The next year the steam fire engine, Blacksnake, arrived. The first Volunteer Fire Company was the Rescue Hook and Ladder Company (Lilly, History of Buchanan County). Photograph courtesy of the St. Joseph Museum

N. R. Penick

On the wagon is driver John Knapp; the boy is Robert Hauck. The man standing (beside the wagon) is John Schafer, and the man in the white uniform is Mark Felling. They are at the Hauck Mill, Second and Franklin streets, built by the Hauck Brothers in 1865. When first built it was called the Excelsior Mill. Later, George Hauck bought out his brother's interest, and the business was organized under the name Hauck Milling Company. The mill was in operation until the 1920s. (Utz, Growth and Development). From an original photograph belonging to Virginia Buck; courtesy of the St. Joseph Museum

The Willard P. Hall home near the corner of Twentieth and Messanie streets. This was Governor Hall's home from 1848 until he died in 1882 at the age of sixty-two years (Boder, St. Joseph Museum Graphic). The photo shows the east facade of the structure. Originally of brick, the exterior has been covered with stucco. A church from 1893 to 1903, it was used from 1903 to 1961 as the rectory of the Sts. Peter and Paul Catholic Church, which can be seen in the background. The building is now vacant. Photograph by Don Reynolds; courtesy of the St. Joseph Museum

This unsigned oil painting of Missouri Governor Willard P. Hall was given to the St. Joseph Museum by Helen and Isabelle Curdy. Willard P. Hall served in the First Missouri Cavalry under Generals Kearney and Alexander Doniphan during the war with Mexico. He was elected to Congress during that tour of duty and then served three additional terms. Elected as Lieutenant Governor, he succeeded to the governorship January 31, 1864, upon the death of Governor Gamble (Boder, St. Joseph Museum Graphic). Governor Hall served until January 1865. Photograph by Don Reynolds; courtesy of the St. Joseph Museum

A depot hack waits on the unpaved street in front of the old Bacon House at the southwest corner of Third and Jules streets. The Bacon House was built in 1866 by John E. Bacon. There was a grocery store on the first floor and a boarding house on the second and third floors. Soon the building was converted to the Bacon Hotel. A fourth floor was eventually added. About 1898, the hotel passed out of the family's hands. The Woodland, Jesse James, and Pioneer hotels later occupied the building (St. Joseph News-Press). Photograph courtesy of the St. Joseph News-Press

The Westminister Presbyterian Church, the stone chapel built in 1866 on the north side of Felix Street near Eighth, became the home for one year for the congregation of the Christ Episcopal Church when the church burned to the ground in 1876 (St. Joseph Museum Graphic). First used for commercial purposes in 1878, the building was occupied by several businesses over the years, including the Bank of Buchanan County during 1911–18. The chapel was torn down by urban renewal in the early 1970s to make way for the new pedestrian mall. Photograph courtesy of the St. Joseph Museum

Townsend and Wall, Sixth and Francis streets. John Townsend and Preston Lowell opened a store called Townsend and Lowell in 1866. A few years later, the name was changed to Townsend and Wood. This partnership was dissolved, and in 1879, Townsend and John Wyatt opened a retail dry goods store under the name of Townsend, Wyatt and Company. The store became the popular meeting place and shopping headquarters for farmers living in a radius of at least fifty miles. Citizens of St. Joseph flocked to the store to supply their household and clothing needs. In 1910, Thomas Wall became a partner, and the store name was changed to Townsend, Wyatt and Wall Dry Goods Company. When the Leader Department Store, which occupied the five-story building that now houses Townsend and Wall, went out of business, Townsend, Wyatt and Wall took a long term lease on the building and moved into it (Utz, Growth and Development). Photograph courtesy of Townsend and Wall and Strathmann Photography

Fannie G. Chisholm Hurst, in her book titled The Four State Chisholm Trail, contends that Thornton Chisholm was the founder of the Chisholm Trail. It was Thornton Chisholm, pictured here, who led the first longhorn cattle herd of 1,800 head to St. Joseph in 1866. They were seven months and ten days getting to St. Joseph (Coy, St. Joseph Museum Graphic). Photograph courtesy of the St. Joseph Museum

The members of Rosenblatt's Band in 1868 were, left to right, standing: Wendelin Wagner, James Blackford, George H. Roll, Herman Rosenblatt, Edmund Hartman, Engelbert Wagner. Sitting: William Berndt, Carl Winkler (director), William Grill, Franz Lorenz. Rosenblatt's Brass Band, founded by Herman Rosenblatt in 1854, was welcomed and encouraged by the people of those days and for many years was famous throughout the West (St. Joseph News–Press). Photograph courtesy of the St. Joseph Museum

Jany 1868.

This photograph of W. A. P. McDonald and his velocipede was made in the late 1860s. He gave several exhibitions in halls and elsewhere in St. Joseph. It was not until about ten years later that the first chain-driven bicycles, with their enormous front wheels, appeared here (St. Joseph News-Press). Photograph courtesy of the St. Joseph News-Press

In Texas, the Comanches and Kiowa Indians meant trouble for the cattle drives, and there was sometimes more Indian trouble in Oklahoma and Kansas. Flooding rivers were also a problem as well as large herds of buffalo. Droughts, cloudbursts, stampedes, as well as terrific hail storms added to the perils of the cattle drive (Coy, St. Joseph Museum Graphic). Photograph from a painting by W. R. Leigh; courtesy of the St. Joseph Museum

"I'se in town Honey!"

Early trademark on the Aunt Jemima Pancake Flour package manufactured in St. Joseph. The Quaker Oats Company in St. Joseph manufactures the pancake flour today, along with a long line of other Quaker products. Photograph courtesy of The Quaker Oats Company

Old mill building, Second and Edmonds streets, St. Joseph. Around 1870, R. T. Davis came to St. Joseph and purchased the City Mills, situated at Third and Antoine streets. In April 1877, he was presented by the citizens with a gold watch "for producing the best flour ever produced in St. Joseph, Missouri," according to Bartlett Boder (St. Joseph Museum Graphic). Davis moved his mill to Second and Edmond streets and enlarged it. He developed a nationally advertised flour known as the Aunt Jemima Pancake Flour which is thought to be the forerunner of all the ready-mixes on supermarket shelves today. One of the great attractions at the World's Fair in Chicago in 1893 was the booth where the prototype of Aunt Jemima herself prepared and dispensed the delicate edibles. Aunt Jemima Pancake Flour was packaged and sold from this old mill building at Second and Edmond streets during the 1890s. The building was demolished in 1970. Photograph courtesy of the St. Joseph Grain Exchange and Strathmann Photography

Corby Chapel (Church of St. John, The Baptist) is located on Route 2, St. Joseph. It was erected by Amanda Corby to the memory of her husband, John, in 1871. "This is perhaps the most elegant and complete structure of the kind in Missouri, while in point of beauty of design, solidity of construction, and tasteful and artistic elegance of finish, it will compare favorably with any similar edifice on the continent. The principal material of which this rare specimen of architectural beauty is constructed is our native limestone . . . . The church is a Gothic structure, built in the shape of a Latin cross. . . . The external appearance of the building is solid and massive, and suggestive of the character of the ecclesiastical architecture of the old world" (Lilly, History of Buchanan County). The bodies of John Corby, his wife, and ten others were buried in a crypt beneath the floor of the chapel. The property went through many transfers, and the bodies were removed to Mount Olivet Cemetery. In 1944, the architectural firm of Eckel & Aldrich, which designed the original chapel, drew plans for remodeling the structure into a residence, now owned and occupied by the Hommel family. Photograph from Rutt, History of Buchanan County

This is how St. Joseph's Co-Cathedral looked prior to remodeling in 1950. The church was constructed in 1871 at a cost of $70,000. Most of the funds for building the church came from Austrian Catholics who were donating funds for building of churches in the United States, then considered "mission territory" (St. Joseph News-Press). Photograph by Don Reynolds; courtesy of the St. Joseph Museum

"BROADWAY" JONES

An advertisement for the Tootle Theatre, "now admitted to be the handsomest theatre in America," shows the auditorium, lobby, and silk plush drop curtain, and lists a few of the many attractions booked for the season of 1897 and 1898.

The Tootle Theatre gave St. Joseph its early fame as one of the most cosmopolitan cities in the country. Photograph from St. Joseph, Missouri, a souvenir booklet by the United Commercial Travelers of America

The Tootle Opera House officially opened December 9, 1872, and thereby introduced St. Joseph society to the exciting and glamorous age of the theatre. The magnificent building, Fifth and Francis, was built by Milton Tootle, Sr., at a cost of $150,000 and was known as the finest theatre west of Chicago. The original theatre contained 1,400 seats, a forty-five foot dome, and twelve sets of scenery. Dressing rooms in the rear of the stage were like "apartments filled with all the comforts and conveniences of home life" (Lilly, History of Buchanan County). Maggie Mitchell, popular star of the 1870s, appeared on opening night; she opened with Fanchon the Cricket. "The spacious building was packed from parquette to gallery with happy people, and from the stage the audience looked like a most colossal and exquisite living bouquet," according to the St. Joseph Daily Gazette.

The famous building hosted the great and near-great names in American stage for the next half-century. It was closed shortly before 1920 when the Dubinsky Brothers entered the theatre business and began staging their own road shows and movies. The building's first floor served as a temporary post office in 1939 when the U.S. Post Office was being replaced. Now called the Pioneer Building, the structure houses professional offices. Photograph courtesy of the St. Joseph Museum

Governor Silas Woodson was the last of the three governors St. Joseph has furnished the state of Missouri. He was elected to that office in 1872, Missouri's first Democratic governor since the Civil War. He took office January 1, 1873, and served until December 1874 (Boder, St. Joseph Museum Graphic). Photograph courtesy of the St. Joseph Museum

By 1873, the original City Hall and Market House had deteriorated to such an extent that Mayor John Severance proposed to erect a new building in the same location. The building shown here was completed in July 1874. It was a handsome building that will be long remembered because of the colorful fruit and vegetable stalls that lined the surrounding sidewalks where marketing and bargaining for the choicest foods were a pleasant part of the day's chores (St. Joseph Museum Graphic). Photograph by Loyal M. Steinel; courtesy of the St. Joseph Museum

Buchanan County's present court house was built 1873-76. Its cost was $173,000, and it is described in history books as "a two-story brick affair, trimmed with stone and erected in cruciform, its arms and legs running east and west and north and south. In the center of the building is a domed rotunda rising 145 feet from the ground level" (St. Joseph News–Press). It was built on the site of the second court house, a high hill donated by Joseph Robidoux.

The building was used for many purposes. There were law offices there. The Latter Day Saints worshipped there. There were even some sleeping rooms. On the second floor, there was a lecture room for the Northwestern Medical College. Part of the structure was used as a large concert hall by the Mendelssohn Society (St. Joseph News-Press).

An 1885 fire caused extensive damage to the interior of the building, and the remodeled dome is shorter than the original. A commemorative volume of the Philadelphia Centennial listed this building as one of the outstanding buildings in the United States. The present restoration, started in 1978, is a long-term project aimed at preserving the classic building. Photograph courtesy of the St. Joseph Museum

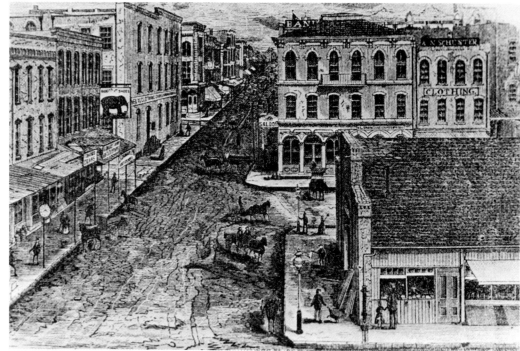

Felix Street in 1873. A portion of the old Market House may be seen, lower right. Photograph from Rutt, History of Buchanan County

"Lunatic Asylum" before the fire. The St. Joseph State Hospital was built in 1872 with the name "State Lunatic Asylum, Number Two." The ultra-Gothic building is shown as it looked in 1875. Five years later, it was destroyed by fire and rebuilt. The asylum was a self-contained world housing a laundry, livery, soap room, kitchens, employee rooms, and complete medical facilities. Treatment for mental patients included sedatives and warm baths, daily walks, and huge breakfasts including: steak, pork chops, potatoes, hominy, and "other very substantial food" (St. Joseph News-Press). The State Hospital later played an important part in the history of psychiatry when some of the earliest work in psychic surgery was done there. Photograph courtesy of the St. Joseph News-Press

Kansas side view of St. Joseph's great "Iron Bridge." Until 1873, there was no bridge across the Missouri River near St. Joseph, and people had to cross on ferry boats. A special election was held January 25, 1871, and the people of St. Joseph voted to authorize the city to issue $500,00 worth of capital stock for the St. Joseph Bridge Building Company. Colonel E. D. Mason was hired as the engineer and a site for the bridge selected. Detroit Bridge and Iron Works submitted the low bid of $710,000, and the first stone was laid September 26, 1871. May 20, 1873, the first locomotive crossed the span pulling a trainload of dignitaries including ex-Governor Hall (Utz, Development and Growth). "The celebration on May 31, marking the completion of the 1,345-foot structure, was one of the grandest ever held in the city. A parade six miles in length wound through the city streets. Then 500 guests attended a special dinner at Tootle and McLaughlin's hall, where the Governor gave the main address. At night, there was dancing in streets lighted by small Japanese lanterns (St. Joseph News-Press). D. S. Mitchell photograph; courtesy of the St. Joseph Museum Collection

Toll House and Iron Bridge, St. Joseph, viewed from the Missouri side. Trains used the center of the span, while buggies and pedestrians traveled on side lanes. The great iron bridge remained the city's only link with Kansas until 1929, when the city opened its new toll-free motor vehicle bridge, now called the Pony Express bridge. Since that date, the original iron bridge has continued to serve only for railroad traffic (St. Joseph News-Press). D. S. Mitchell photograph; courtesy of the St. Joseph Museum Collection

The James Kay home at Sixth and
Felix streets, no longer standing. The
Kay family lived here for twenty-
eight years. The picture was made
about 1875. Photograph courtesy of
the St. Joseph Museum

1860-1880

John Severance became postmaster in 1875, and the post office was moved to the southeast corner of Second and Francis streets. Frank Tracy was appointed postmaster in 1881, and he moved the post office to the Tootle Theatre Building. The post office was next moved to the Tootle building east of the opera house, and in 1891 to its permanent location at Eighth and Edmond streets (St. Joseph Museum Graphic). Photograph by D. S. Mitchell; courtesy of the St. Joseph Museum

The entire crew of the J. W. Ambrose Foundry was photographed in 1875 while standing by the plant, near Eighth and Monterey streets. The brick portion of the building, at the left, is still standing in the former Union Depot yards north of Monterey, between Sixth and Eighth streets. Photograph courtesy of the St. Joseph News-Press

When Joseph Robidoux had the city of St. Joseph mapped out, he gave a half-block for a Market Square. This 1875 photograph shows the east side (north half) of Market Square. Photograph by D. S. Mitchell; courtesy of the St. Joseph Museum

Felix Street in 1875, showing the buildings of the Merchants Insurance Company and Senate Saloon and Restaurant, 110 and 112 Felix. Photograph by D. S. Mitchell; courtesy of the St. Joseph Museum

Shares in the Henry Krug Packing Company sold for $100 each in 1904. Photograph courtesy of the St. Joseph Museum

Henry Krug Packing Company was established in the winter of 1877-78. It was a thriving packing house for almost twenty years (Frank Popplewell, St. Joseph, Missouri as a Center of the Cattle Trade). Upper left: packing house; upper right; killing room; bottom left: dressing room; bottom right: shipping room (St. Joseph and Northwest Missouri).

In 1846, John Corby had established the city's first "slaughtering house," as early meat-packing plants were called. By 1861, three more were operating in the heart of the city. Krug and Company went farther south, at Fourth and Monterey streets. Photograph from St. Joseph and Northwest Missouri, Illustrated Souvenir Edition of the St. Joseph Daily News

This is a view of Smith Park in 1877. The view is to the northwest from Twelfth and Francis streets. Smith Park, now a part of the Civic Center, was the pride of St. Joseph. In the center was a statue of a Doctor Cogswell, a temperance advocate who had donated similar statues to other cities in the United States. A feature of the statue was a drinking fountain--providing water only. A few years later, when the statue turned green, the city fathers removed it from the park (St. Joseph News–Press). Photograph courtesy of the St. Joseph News–Press

It was not until 1870 that firemen in St. Joseph were paid, and in 1873 a second steam fire engine was purchased, the Blue Bird. In 1875, the St. Joseph Fire Company was justly proud of the Blue Bird, which was trimmed with German silver and nickel fittings. The pumper was needed because there was no water system and water had to be pumped from the nearest well in order to put out fires. Photograph by D. S. Mitchell; photograph courtesy of the St. Joseph Museum

The F. Wenz Shoe Company occupied the first floor of this building at 223-225 Edmond Street when this picture was made in 1878. The little fellow in the hat is Fred J. Wenz. The top floor was occupied by R. Uhlman's Photographic Gallery (St. Joseph News–Press). Photograph courtesy of the St. Joseph News–Press

In 1888, Mary Alicia Owen made important discoveries in voodoo magic. At one time, she was president of the American Folklore Society. She investigated the rites and customs of the American Indians, especially the Sac Indians who had formerly occupied the territory north of St. Joseph. She was taken into tribal membership in 1882 and joined some of their secret societies. She was the author of many books concerning Indian history (Boder, St. Joseph Museum Graphic). Photograph courtesy of the St. Joseph Museum

The three Owen sisters secured for themselves an almost international reputation, not only in folklore and local history but in geology as well. Luella Owen painted in water colors, probably in the 1870s, these portraits of her two sisters and herself which were presented to the St. Joseph Museum by John Cargill. Miss Luella, pictured here, was also a fearless explorer of caves and a geologist of international fame. She was inducted into the American Geographic Society at the same session when Admiral Robert E. Perry was admitted. This membership entitled her to travel throughout the world without a passport (Boder, St. Joseph Museum Graphic). Photograph courtesy of the St. Joseph Museum

Juliette Owen was the youngest of the sisters. She worked in water colors. Her chosen scientific fields were ornithology and botany, and she was the author of several books in those fields (Boder, St. Joseph Museum Graphic). Photograph courtesy of the St. Joseph Museum

Leaving St. Joseph for Leadville, 1879, at Eighth and Edmond streets. Photograph courtesy of the St. Joseph Museum

The building which housed The Daily Evening News is in the upper center of this composite photograph. Upper left shows the business office; upper right; the editor's room; and bottom center, the press room. May 3, 1879, The Daily Evening News was started by Judge A. Royal and George H. Cross in the structure that was the home of The Western News. The building was located at the southeast corner of Fourth and Francis streets. The paper was relocated at 416 Felix Street, changed hands, and changed its name to The St. Joseph Daily News. In 1903, a company was organized and purchased The Daily News and The Evening Press and united the papers under the name of The St. Joseph News and Press. In 1905, the paper became The St. Joseph News–Press. In 1913, The St. Joseph News–Press moved to its present location at Ninth and Edmond streets (The St. Joseph News–Press). Photograph from St. Joseph and Northwest Missouri

The St. Joseph Museum, Eleventh and Charles streets, is a Gothic-style sandstone structure containing approximately 21,000 square feet of floor space, 43 large rooms, and 3,600 square feet of beautifully landscaped grounds. It includes a square block of city property. Built as a residence in 1879 by William M. Wyeth, the building later was purchased by the widow of another early pioneer, Milton Tootle. At the time of the Goetz purchase, in 1947, the building was owned by the Tootle estate. The Tootle family has also been a strong supporter of the St. Joseph Museum (St. Joseph Museum Graphic). Photograph courtesy of the St. Joseph Museum

chapter 7
Jesse James

S t. Joseph has been called the town where the Pony Express got its start and Jesse James met his end. It has been said, too, that, in the history of the United States, few men have achieved more widespread fame for less praiseworthy accomplishments than have Jesse James and his brother, Frank. Adept in outwitting the law, from 1866 to 1882, the Jameses established a world's record in keeping out of its clutches. Both boys were born in Kearney, Missouri, near St. Joseph. It was their avocation to rob banks and railroad trains, not ignoring an occasional stagecoach. They did not confine their activities to Missouri alone, but also made raids into Kansas, Iowa, Minnesota, and Kentucky.

Jesse James was the most dangerous of all the border bandits because he was the most desperate. Eternal vigilance was the price he had to pay for his liberty. Under the disguise of "Mr. Howard," Jesse and his family moved to St. Joseph in 1881. Little did the people of St. Joseph realize that the quiet, church-going man was the notorious outlaw Jesse James. His career came to an end in 1882 when he was shot in the base of the skull in his home by Robert Ford, a twenty-year-old whom Jesse had trusted and befriended (Chamber of Commerce brochure).

Jesse James as he appeared about the time of his marriage in 1874. The only copy of this picture during Jesse's lifetime was the single copy which Mrs. Zerelda Samuels, his mother, wore as a pendant around her neck. It was the last adult picture taken of him and is owned by the St. Joseph Museum (St. Joseph Museum Graphic). Photograph courtesy of the St. Joseph Museum

Frank James, brother of Jesse James, 1883. Photograph courtesy of the St. Joseph Museum

Mrs. Zerelda Samuels, mother of Jesse and Frank James. Photograph courtesy of the St. Joseph Museum

This house at 1002 South Twenty-First Street was occupied by Jesse James, his wife, and their two children from November 8, 1881, until December 24, 1881. (St. Joseph Museum Graphic). Photograph courtesy of the St. Joseph Museum and Strathmann Photography

The Second Presbyterian Church was at the northwest corner of Twelfth and Penn streets, cat-a-corner from the famous World's Hotel. Jesse James took his children to Sunday School classes at this church each Sunday and returned for them when classes were over. Jesse, the son of a Baptist preacher, was very religious, could quote extensively from the Bible, and could pray aloud in meeting imploring forgiveness for his sins (St. Joseph Museum Graphic). The Second Presbyterian Church is now located at Thirty-Third and Penn streets. Photograph courtesy of the St. Joseph Museum

Bob Ford was twenty years old when he shot Jesse James. He used the 45-calibre pearl-handled Smith and Wesson revolver which he had received as a present from Jesse James. Ford shot James in the back of the head. James was on a chair dusting off a picture on the wall of a room in his home when the fatal bullet passed through his head and entered the wall. Visitors today can still see the bullet hole. In 1939, the James home was moved to the Belt Highway as a tourist attraction. The house was purchased in 1977 by Mr. and Mrs. Robert Keatley and donated to the Pony Express Historical Association. It was moved back to its original neighborhood near Patee House and today is a complete Jesse James Museum, featuring many original furnishings and articles from the days of Jesse James. Photograph from the Lozo Collection; courtesy of the St. Joseph Museum

This picture shows the crowds gathering around the Jesse James house, 1318 Lafayette, the morning he was shot to death, April 3, 1882 (from a sketch in Leslie's Weekly; presented to the St. Joseph Museum by the Central Public Library, St. Joseph). The hilltop, one-story house also had sheds and a stable down hill at the rear. The James family moved to the house in November, accompanied by the trusted Charley Ford. Charley Ford went to the home of his mother in Kearney just eight days before Jesse was shot and brought back his brother Bob Ford, who shot Jesse James. Photograph courtesy of the St. Joseph Museum

The two children of Jesse James, three-year-old daughter, Mary, and seven-year-old son, Jesse Edwards James. On the funeral train southbound for Kearney, Missouri, from Cameron, they slept on the seat beside their silent mother. The train was a freight to which the single-passenger coach was attached, and the coffin bearing Jesse James in his shroud was tied on the rear platform. The members of the James family kept a sharp watch on the coffin for fear the body would be stolen. The funeral service was held at the New Hope Baptist church near Kearney, and the body was buried on his mother's farm. Some years later, the body was removed to Kearney's cemetery. (St. Joseph Museum Graphic). Photograph courtesy of the St. Joseph Museum

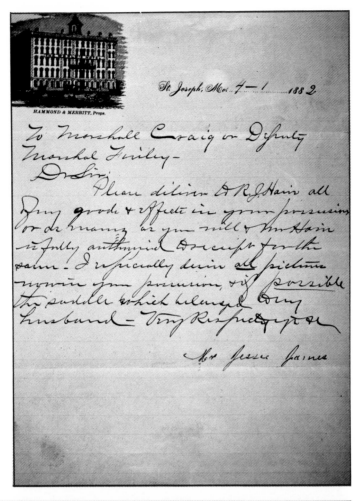

This letter from Mrs. Jesse James was among the papers given to the St. Joseph Museum by Mrs. Mort H. Craig. The World's Hotel (letterhead) was formerly the Patee House and was two blocks south of the house where Jesse James was shot. The letter was addressed to Marshal Craig or Deputy Marshal Finley and asked that they deliver to R. J. Hain the goods and effects in their possession which belonged to her late husband. She especially desired all photographs and the saddle (St. Joseph Museum Graphic). Photograph courtesy of the St. Joseph Museum

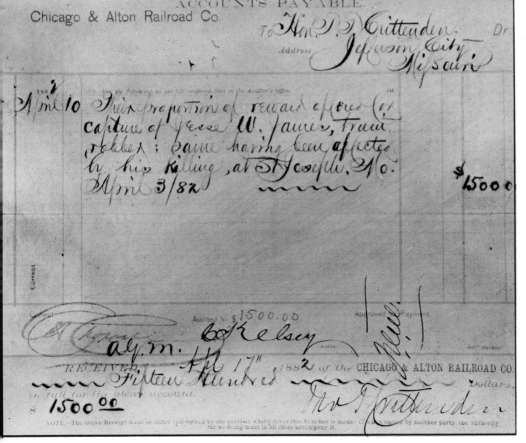

The Alton railroad paid its proportion of the reward money to Governor Crittenden. It was the $10,000 reward offered by Governor Crittenden for the capture of Jesse and Frank James and the immunity and pardon promised those of his followers who would betray him that brought an end to that charmed career of the world's most famous bandit. The money was furnished the Governor by various railroads and express companies (Bartlett Boder, St. Joseph Museum Graphic). Photograph courtesy of the St. Joseph Museum

chapter 8

Eugene Field

S t. Joseph is closely associated with the intimate life of the famous poet and newspaper journalist Eugene Field. It was here that he found his loved one, wooed and wed her—fourteen-year-old Julia Comstock, who lived with her parents at Fifth and Isadore streets. It was here the newlyweds lived a part of their lives at 425 North Eleventh Street. Both of the residences are still standing. It was here the young couple's first two children were born. The death of his first-born, a son, filled Field's heart with a sorrow that inspired the tenderest of all his poems, "Little Boy Blue."

Field served as city editor of the *St. Joseph Gazette* in 1875-76 and endeared himself to St. Joseph with his pranks, his brilliant quips, and his genius. In turn, Field regarded the city with great affection, as evidenced by his poems "St. Jo Gazette" and "Lover's Lane, Saint Jo," the latter written in 1889 in London. Field was in ill health and his doctor sent him there to rest and recuperate. Alone in the foggy and dingy old city, he and Julia relived the days of their courtship in St. Joseph when they meandered slowly down a lovely lane, their first kiss, their troth to each other . . . , and "Lover's Lane, Saint Jo" was penned.

Field died of a heart attack in his sleep in Chicago in 1895. He was found dead in his bed with a gas light burning and an open book beside him. Today, he and Julia lay buried side-by-side in the Cloister Close of the Church of the Holy Comforter in Chicago.

Eugene Field as he appeared in 1875 when he "ran the local" on the St. Joseph Gazette. Field returned to St. Louis in 1876 as an editorial writer on the St. Louis Journal and Times. He later worked on newspapers in Kansas City, Denver, and Chicago. Photograph from the Lozo Collection; courtesy of the St. Joseph Museum

Julia Comstock (Mrs. Eugene) Field as she appeared when the Field family resided in Chicago in the early 1890s. Photograph presented to the Museum by Ruth Field Foster, daughter of Julia and Eugene Field; courtesy of the St. Joseph Museum

Eugene Field and Julia Comstock "snailed along the leafy aisles of Lover's Lane in a stanch but squeaky chaise, with her head upon his shoulder and his arm around her so...."

"Lover's Lane" was a dirt country road (not paved until 1914) north of St. Joseph when Eugene Field courted Julia Comstock. It was then known as Rochester Road because it went to Rochester, Missouri. It was a pretty road with large trees shading it, sections of rail fence, and growths of alders, willows, and other wild shrubs. It was also a lonely road and a favorite of young lovers. After writing "Lover's Lane, Saint Jo," in London, Eugene Field returned to this country and made his last visit to St. Joseph in 1895. He gave readings of his poems at the YWCA music hall, and it is reported that St. Joseph loved "Lover's Lane, Saint Jo." In 1897, a city ordinance was enacted which described and named the city's streets, and this country lane officially became Lovers Lane. The area was annexed to the city in 1889. Photograph from the collection of Nellie Loubey; courtesy of Strathmann Photography

> But if again that angel train
> And golden-head come back to me
> To bear me to Eternity,
> My watching will not be in vain.
>
> The first verse I ever wrote.
> 1878
>
> Eugene Field

"The first verse I ever wrote, 1878," according to the pen of Eugene Field himself. This is a reproduction of an early lithograph originally showing Eugene Field and the poem. It was done in Chicago in the early 1890s by Henry Taylor, Jr., a friend of Eugene Field and a well-known artist. Photograph courtesy of the St. Joseph Museum

The little toy dog
    is covered with dust,
But sturdy and staunch
    he stands,
And the little toy soldier
    is red with rust,
And his musket moulds
    in his hands.
Time was when the little
    toy dog was new,
And the soldier was
    passing fair;
And that was the time when
    our Little Boy Blue
Kissed them and
    put them there.

The statue of "Little Boy Blue" was presented to the St. Joseph Public Library, Tenth and Felix streets, in 1943 by members of the St. Joseph Women's Press Club. "Little Boy Blue" is perhaps one of Field's best known poems. Field so loved children that into the poem he poured all his tenderness, his understanding, and his sympathy. Its appeal to human hearts soon made the poem known and loved around the world. *Photograph courtesy of the St. Joseph Museum*

Carrie Comstock, standing, and Ida Comstock, sitting, sisters of Julia Comstock Field, taken in the early 1870s. The Comstocks lived at Fifth and Isadore streets, where Field met his future wife, fourteen-year-old Julia (St. Joseph Museum Graphic). *Photograph from the Lozo Collection; courtesy of the St. Joseph Museum*

According to Seward Lilly (History of Buchanan County), the Pacific House was built in the winter of 1859-60 on the corner of Third and Francis streets at a cost of $120,000. At that time, its principal front was on Francis Street. In 1868, it was totally destroyed by fire. It was rebuilt the following year with its main front on Third Street. Eugene and his bride had their wedding breakfast at Pacific House October 17, 1873, for seventy persons. "Oysters in every style, steaks, turkeys, quail, prairie chickens, and 'rivers of champagne' were served. Field then invited the wedding party to St. Louis. Most of them accepted and the merrymaking continued there" (Boder, St. Joseph Museum Graphic). *Photograph courtesy of the St. Joseph Museum*

chapter 9
1880-1900

St. Joseph has been called a boom or bust town. The 1880s and the Gay Nineties was definitely a boom period and is often referred to as the Golden Age of St. Joseph. The Union Pacific began to run trains into the city, and St. Joseph's position on the rail routes was established. The city developed into a major wholesale distributor center for the western United States and moved full steam ahead. A fresh impetus was given industries by the revival on a gigantic scale of the meat-packing industry, and St. Joseph became one of the principal packing centers in the United States.

The newly rich began constructing mansion-like residences, many with stone fortress-like walls, stained-glass windows, turrets, and towers reminiscent of the old castles along the Rhine. Like pictures from a book of fairy tales, many magnificent buildings of that era still stand in the city and record by their elegance the climate of confidence and optimism prevalent in St. Joseph at that period.

As homes and businesses increased in number, the need for more municipal services increased. The city sewer system got under way in the 1880s. In the same decade, the St. Joseph Water Company built its plant north of the city and extended mains to the most densely populated areas.

Houses extended farther away from the downtown area, so a system of public transportation was necessary. Omnibus lines were started using wagons, carriages, and buggies pulled by horses. Steel tracks were installed, and the horse-drawn streetcar became popular. By 1889, St. Joseph had electric streetcars—the first city in the nation to operate them on a regular schedule. Electric lighting for the town came later.

As living conditions improved, so did the quality of the city's recreation. St. Joseph sponsored a spectacular 1889 Exposition at fairgrounds located where the present Mark Twain and Truman Middle schools are located. The Exposition was housed in the 990-foot-long St. Joseph Steel Car plant, but a disastrous fire two weeks after opening night bankrupted the Steel Car Company, and many businessmen lost their exhibits at the fair. It also ended plans to hold a World's Fair in St. Joseph in 1890.

Another popular recreational spot just developing was Lake Contrary, a resort in the southwestern part of the city served by both streetcar lines and railroads.

The St. Joseph Water Company laying the water mains (St. Joseph and Northwest Missouri, 1894). Photograph from St. Joseph and Northwest Missouri

The latest in delivery service was available at Webb's Drug Store. Deliveries were made twenty-four hours a day. Photograph courtesy of the St. Joseph News-Press

This is a photograph of the St. Joseph Water Company's first pumping station on Waterworks Road northwest of the city. In December 1879, a contract was let to the St. Joseph Water Company to build the waterworks. They were to secure pressure through the gravity system, which meant that the tanks or reservoirs would have to be placed on high hills so that the water would run downhill into the hydrants and homes (Utz, Growth and Development). Photograph courtesy of the St. Joseph Water Company

An early view of Webb's Drug Store, Tenth and Pacific streets, shows one of the first soda fountains in the city—and with a marble top, no less. O. O. Turner, later a South Side drug store owner, is behind the counter.

According to the St. Joseph News-Press, William Webb came to St. Joseph in the 1870s and went to work at a drug store for two dollars a week. Thirty-five years later he had acquired four drug stores, becoming owner of the Webb Drug Store in 1880. In addition to being one of the first druggists to put in a soda fountain, he was also one of the first druggists to serve lunches. The Webb Drug Store was best known for its homemade ice cream.

Webb never believed in selling liquors. He kept some on hand during Prohibition for medicinal prescriptions but had to give that up—too many of his friends developed sudden and prolonged illnesses. Photograph courtesy of the St. Joseph News-Press

THE PRESENT UNION STATION

THE FIRST UNION STATION

The Englehart-Davison Mercantile Company building, 212-214 North Fourth Street, was established in 1880. The photograph was taken circa 1927. The building is in Wholesale Row and is listed in the National Register of Historic Places. Photograph from St. Joseph Today

The first Union Depot, a building erected across Mitchell Avenue with a frontage of 405 feet on Sixth Street, was completed April 30, 1882. The upper story was arranged for a hotel. The first train to leave the Union Depot was over the Union Pacific route. On the night of February 9, 1895, the depot was destroyed by fire. During the same year, a new building was erected upon the site of the old one, with many improvements. The new Union Depot, opened for business in January 1896 (Rutt, History of Buchanan County), was closed and demolished in the 1950s. Photograph from Rutt, History of Buchanan County

Missouri River front, foot of Messanie Street, 1894. Photograph from St. Joseph and Northwest Missouri

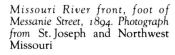

Third Street, looking south from Edmond, circa 1887. The Merchant's Bank may be seen on the corner. The Nave and McCord Mercantile Company, grocers, shown at 310 South Third, were established in 1857 (Lilly, History of Buchanan County). Photograph from Illustrated Review of St. Joseph, Missouri

The R. L. McDonald & Company, selling dry goods, notions, and gent's furnishings, began wholesaling in 1866 (Lilly, History of Buchanan County). In 1880, the company was able to move into their imposing new building at Fourth and Francis streets. The company closed in the 1920s, and the building was later occupied by the Big Smith Work Clothing Company. The building was later acquired by PALMCO. After extensive renovation on the inside and outside, the building was named "The Landmark." It is listed in the National Register of Historic Places. Photograph from St. Joseph and Northwest Missouri

In the mid-1880s and in the vicinity of Fifth and Felix streets, G. W. Chase is shown in his vendor's wagon selling fruits, produce, and confectionery items. This was the forerunner of the Chase Candy Company, which started in 1876 and operated in the downtown district for many years. The company is now in operation at 3600 Leonard Road. Note the dirt street, brick gutter, and the workday attire of the men pictured. Photograph owned by W. Ray Highsmith

102

The YMCA Building at the north-east corner of Seventh and Felix was constructed in 1887. It had an auditorium that later became the Colonial Theatre (St. Joseph News–Press). The structure, razed in the urban renewal program in the 1970s, was then known as the Schneider Building. In 1910, the YMCA was moved to another headquarters at Tenth and Faraon streets; this building was razed in 1979 when the YMCA moved into its new building at 315 South Sixth Street. Photograph courtesy of Nellie Loubey and Strathmann Photography

This photograph shows the interior of the Englehart-Davison Mercantile Company's building. "Braids from Italy, Switzerland and Japan, unfinished straw bodies from Manila, felt bodies from Czechoslovakia, silks, velvets, and ornaments from France and Germany, these and other carefully selected materials assembled from many far-off lands are shaped from skilled fingers of scores of St. Joseph girls into many hats of attractive design at the Englehart-Davison Company" (St. Joseph Today). Photograph from St. Joseph Today

The first shop building and craftsmen of the D. H. Schmidt Carriage and Wagon Works are pictured behind the original buildings at Ninth and Lafayette, the site the company has occupied up to the present time. The photograph, taken from east of Ninth Street, also shows the old Electric Hotel, the brick building just north of the wagon shop. At lower left can be seen a portion of a wooden sidewalk, a necessity since concrete and brick walks had not been built.

When Dietrich Henry Schmidt started the business in 1885, the firm made wagons, carriages, and buggies of all types. When motorized vehicles came along, the firm shifted to making automobile and truck bodies, and today it also handles a wide variety of repair work. Photograph courtesy of the St. Joseph Museum

According to the Illustrated Review of St. Joseph, Missouri, *the St. Joseph Natatorium, a popular health resort at the corner of Fifth and Jule streets, opened May 1, 1886. The swimming pool, 40-by-100 feet with a capacity of 280,000 gallons, was supplied with water from the Missouri River, which was constantly running into it at the rate of three gallons per minute. In addition to swimming, there could be had baths of all kinds, and the manager of the pool gave swimming lessons (Mondays and Fridays were reserved for the ladies). Hazel Faubion (Tales of old "St. Joe") says the Natatorium closed in 1889 and the building was occupied by the Bijou Theatre, which operated about four years until it was partially destroyed by fire. It was rebuilt and became the Crawford Theatre. In 1899, it changed hands, was renovated, and became the Lyceum Theatre. After the Lyceum closed in 1927, the building was used as a parking garage. It was razed in connection with the demolition of the Robidoux Hotel to make way for a business complex in 1976. Photograph from Illustrated Review*

Bartlett Boder is identified by an arrow in this school group picture probably taken in the late 1800s. The schoolhouse location cannot be identified. Photograph courtesy of the St. Joseph Museum

This is a photograph of the Chamber of Commerce Building on the corner of Third and Edmond streets, "equipped with passenger elevators and all conveniences of a metropolitan office building," about 1888. The Board of Trade, organized October 19, 1878, occupied part of the building. "The Board of Trade is one of the most efficient organizations of its kind in the West. The membership is composed of nearly 250 representatives of all classes of business and professional men. . . . Scarcely a day passes that the Board of Trade does not direct some act of importance bearing upon the direct interests of the city—better mail service, complaint of freight rate discrimination, delegates from neighboring towns received in behalf of enterprises in St. Joseph. . . . Ten years ago, before the Board of Trade was organized, St. Joseph had scarcely a dozen enterprises. In 1887, the city has 170 of all kinds (Illustrated Review). In 1892, the Board of Trade merged with the Commercial Club. In 1917, the Commercial Club took the name of St. Joseph Chamber of Commerce (St. Joseph News-Press). Photograph from Illustrated Review

The Swift and Company Plant in the St. Joseph Stock Yards. The St. Joseph Stock Yards Company was organized in 1886. The tract of land chosen for the site contained 413 acres south of the city near the Missouri River. Construction of the yards and the Exchange Building was completed in 1887. St. Joseph is in a major livestock feeding area, and the new railroads provided good connections with the source of cattle supply and with eastern markets. It was due to the efforts of John Donovan, who was developing the southern part of the city, that Gustavus F. Swift of Chicago came to St. Joseph in 1896 and purchased 80 percent of the entire property of the St. Joseph Stock Yards Company. In 1898, the Swift and Company plant opened for business. Other plants soon followed (Popplewell, Cattle Trade). Photograph from Show Me

The Verdi Mandolin Club, organized March 17, 1886, gave many delightful entertainments at home and in surrounding cities, using mostly classical music (St. Joseph and Northwest Missouri). Left to right, back row: O. J. Albrecht, J. A. Riemenschneider; front row: C. L. Horn, H. E. Evans, C. T. Cloudas, W. A. Scott. Photograph from St. Joseph and Northwest Missouri

Dr. Hall's Sanitarium And Turkish Bath, corner of Third and Faraon streets. The building was constructed of brick, had forty rooms, and was three stories high. It was advertised in the Illustrated Review as "A Health Resort and Water Cure." The ad further explains: "By use of the Turkish and other hot air baths, the patient experiences the benefits derived from the Hot Springs. The tonic and invigorating influence of sea bathing can be enjoyed and benefits derived by the ocean brine baths. Patients can receive benefits obtained by a visit to the mountains, or the springs, or sea shore in visiting Dr. Hall's Sanitarium" (Illustrated Review). Photograph from Illustrated Review

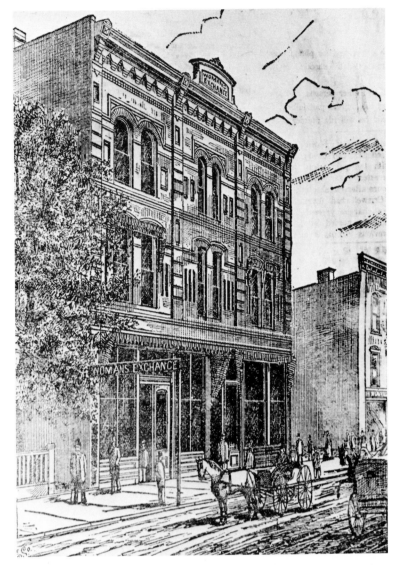

"According to a publication of the times, the Woman's Exchange was organized in March 1886 as a result of the concerted efforts of a number of benevolent ladies of St. Joseph. Its purpose was to provide a place where woman's work of every kind that was purchasable could be placed for sale.

"Offered for sale were paintings and other decorative works, breads, rolls, beaten biscuits, doughnuts, cakes, jars of fruits, pickles, jellies, and preserves.

"The place was popular. In July of that year sales zoomed to $92.00, of which the association kept 10 percent or $9.20.

"The Woman's Exchange also served lunches daily at twenty-five cents each and boasted that no place in the city surpassed their lunches at the price. Was the luncheon business profitable? Goodness, yes. The lunches for the third week in July netted $16.00.

"A city directory of 1889 lists the location of the Woman's Exchange as 514 Francis Street. The building has long been gone.

"The artist has faithfully copied a photograph of the era. Photoengraving hadn't been invented then, so this steel engraving is the only available picture" (St. Joseph News-Press). Photograph courtesy of the St. Joseph News-Press

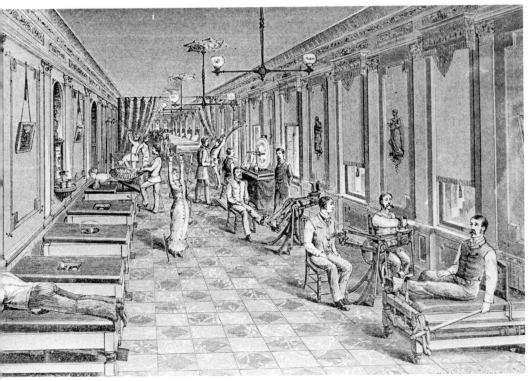

This is an interior view of Dr. Hall's Mechanical Massage room for "the treatment of diseases by rapid vibrations." His advertisement in the Illustrated Review explains: "Mechanical massage is a process to make people well and strong by thoroughly exercising the muscles of the body. The vibratory treatment is beneficial and curative in insomnia, headaches, neuralgia, rheumatism, paralysis, general debility, neurasthenia, and all bodily conditions where the forces of nature are at low ebb. Open to gentlemen 8 A.M. to 12 P.M. and 7 to 9 P.M. Ladies' hours 1 to 6 P.M." Photograph from Illustrated Review

St. Joseph once had a home for aged and dependent ex-slaves of the U.S.A. In 1887, a brick house at Seventeenth and Highland was built for the slaves and operated for two years (Rutt, History of Buchanan County). Many of the slaves were more than 100 years old, had no known relatives living, and were wholly dependent upon the charity of the people. A preliminary report on the Eighth Census of the year 1860 showed Buchanan County had 21,799 whites with 101 free Negroes and 2,011 Negro slaves (Coy, St. Joseph Museum Graphic). Photograph courtesy of the St. Joseph Museum

This is a photograph of the Benton Club House, Seventh and Faraon streets. June 8, 1887, papers of incorporation of the Benton Club House Company were filed at the Buchanan County Court House. The purpose of the corporation was to "purchase, to sell, to own, use and occupy Real Estate for the mutual profit of the members thereof." On June 10, 1887, the Benton Club House Company purchased for $20,000 the two lots and three houses on the northwest corner of Seventh and Faraon streets. The buildings were remodeled, and the St. Joseph newspapers reported that "The Club House is unsurpassed in its appointments and is one of the finest in the entire West. The halls and billiard room have inlaid floors, easy couches, cozy arm chairs, and everything for comfort." During the many years of its life, the Club has been a comfortable and pleasant gathering place for many St. Joseph families and their friends (Sheridan Logan, Old Saint Jo, Gateway to the West). The Club is still in existence today. Photograph courtesy of the St. Joseph Museum

Dr. A. V. Banes Medicine Company's Offices and Warehouse, 223 North Fifth Street. According to the Illustrated Review, "Dr. Banes has the largest practice of any physician in the West." One of his advertisements for "Dr. A. V. Banes' Nine O'Clock Pills" in the Illustrated Review reads: "If you have a disordered liver causing costive bowels or yellow skin which has resulted in distressing piles or do your kidneys refuse to perform? The Nine O'Clock Pill will soon relieve the clogged condition of your system and make you feel like a new man. Only 25 cents. Sent by mail." Another one of his ads proclaims: "Dr. A. V. Banes' Rheumatic Specific will stop a rheumatic pain in 24 hours. Your druggist has it— $1. Are you sick? Write to Dr. A. V. Banes, 5 and Jules, St. Joe, Mo. He has prescribed the same in his professional practice here for the past 23 years with success." Photograph from Illustrated Review

Dr. John A. French entered practice in St. Joseph in 1880. In 1888, he erected at 402-406 South Eighth Street the St. Joseph School and Hospital for Training Nurses. The next picture shows the site where Dr. French erected his Sanitarium for Nervous Diseases. The bottom picture shows Dr. French at his residence. Photograph from Rutt, History of Buchanan County

DR. A. V. BANES MEDICINE CO.'S OFFICES AND WAREROOMS, 223 N. FIFTH STREET.

St. Joseph School and Hospital for Training Nurses

The Site of Dr. French's Sanitarium for Nervous Diseases

RESIDENCE OF JOHN A. FRENCH, M.D.

This picture was made in 1888 by the late Huston Wyeth at his summer home at the southeast corner of 36th Street and Frederick Avenue. His son is shown wearing kilts, and a liveried coachman is on the driver's seat. Frederick Avenue was then a dirt road. The house burned September 30, 1899, according to the St. Joseph News-Press. Photograph courtesy of the St. Joseph News-Press

The bank of Tootle, Lemon & Company was organized in 1889 and located at the northwest corner of Sixth and Francis streets. It became the Tootle-Lemon National Bank in 1902 and the Tootle-Lacy National Bank 1918. In 1955, the name was changed to Tootle National Bank. In 1960, it merged with the Empire Trust Company and in 1963 merged with the American National. The American National now occupies the lower floors of Robidoux Center. Photograph from a watercolor painting; courtesy of the St. Joseph Museum

"This street scene at Second and Francis Street is from a steel engraving made from a photograph before 1890. The big building at the extreme right is the old Pacific House, later the Metropole Hotel and razed about 1940. The city's traffic problems were becoming acute. . . . Note the team and wagon near the center. The horses have been 'parked' headed in the wrong direction, blocking a pedestrian crossing—and are without a driver. Maybe he is inside purchasing some wood window blinds which are made in the factory at the corner. Maybe he has slipped down the street for 'a quick one.' At any rate, the driver at the right has had to pull over to the wrong side of the street" (St. Joseph News-Press). Photograph courtesy of the St. Joseph News-Press

This drawing shows the resurfacing of the streets with asphaltic concrete, then termed "asphaltum." This view, made south of the old City Hall, appeared in a publication printed in St. Joseph in the 1880s. An accompanying article pointed out that Paris, London, and Montreal, as well as St. Joseph, were among many cities using the new paving material (St. Joseph News-Press). Photograph courtesy of the St. Joseph News-Press

"Felix Street, east from Fourth, as it appeared to an artist in 1887. Felix Street had a traffic problem even in those days. Apparently there was no parking (or hitching) on the north side of the street. There were no traffic lights, of course. Streetlights were gas although there were a few electric lights over the city. The building at the right still looks much the same as it did when the artist made this drawing. It was the State Savings Bank but is now known as the Missouri Valley Trust Company building. The corner at the left was the location of a clothing store. Unsightly telephone poles were in prominence then but now are gone in favor of underground cables" (St. Joseph News-Press). Photograph courtesy of the St. Joseph News-Press

"This is the corner of Fifth and Francis streets as it appeared in 1887. The Tootle Opera House is the imposing building shown. Note the gas lamp on the corner. There is one unusual sight in the picture; the horse is headed east. It has been many years since any eastbound traffic has been allowed on Francis Street" (St. Joseph News-Press). Photograph from a steel etching; courtesy of the St. Joseph News-Press

114

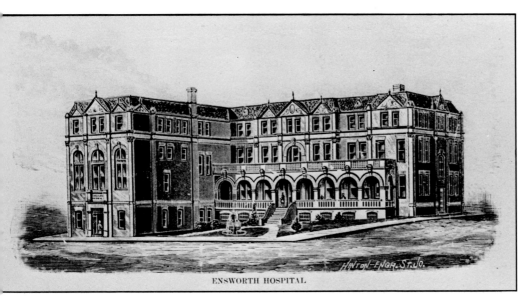

ENSWORTH HOSPITAL

The Ensworth Hospital, Seventh and Jule streets, circa 1888. The St. Joseph Medical College and the College of Physicians and Surgeons, two early medical schools in St. Joseph, merged, and the new institution was called the Samuel Ensworth Medical College in honor of the man who gave $100,000 to build a school and hospital. The Ensworth Hospital, a three-story brick building, was opened in 1888. The institution was later taken over by the Methodist Episcopal Church. Eventually, the building proved too small and inadequate. The northeast corner at Eighth and Faraon streets was purchased and a modern four-story hospital erected in 1924. Photograph from St. Joseph Today

MISSOURI.—VIEWS IN THE CITY OF ST. JOSEPH, A GROWING METROPOLIS OF THE SOUTHWEST.

"Views in the city of St. Joseph, a growing metropolis of the Southwest":
(1) Chamber of Commerce
(2) City Hall
(3) Third Street, looking south
(4) Buchanan County Court House
(5) Merchants Bank
(6) View of St. Joseph, looking up the Missouri River
(7) Academy of the Sacred Heart
(8) Steel Railway Bridge over the Missouri River
(9) Public Institution, Number Two
Photograph from Harper's Weekly, 1888; courtesy of the St. Joseph Museum

William Hackett Lewis is shown here as an officer in the elite Craig Rifles of St. Joseph. His unit was later attached to the Fourth Missouri Regiment, Missouri National Guard, commanded by Colonel Joseph A. Corby (St. Joseph Museum Graphic). This photograph was taken in the 1880s. Photograph courtesy of the St. Joseph Museum

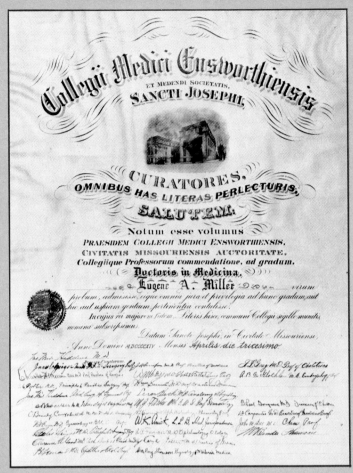

Dr. Eugene A. Miller received this diploma when he graduated from Ensworth Medical College in 1914. It was the last graduating class (Boder, St. Joseph Museum Graphic). Photograph courtesy of the St. Joseph Museum

These St. Joseph physicians were brought together May 1, 1931, for a final picture before the old Ensworth Hospital was razed. They are, left to right, front row: Doctor J. W. Mays, William E. Pentz, J. H. Sampson, W. T. Elam, Paul Forgrave, Jacob Geiger, A. L. Gray, J. J. Reynolds, Leroi Beck, Charles Geiger, A. E. Burger, A. A. Disque, C. H. Branson, G. A. Lau, M. S. Gray, W. L. Kenny, Louis Bauman, Eugene A. Miller, and Julius Kangisser (Boder, St. Joseph Museum Graphic). Photograph courtesy of the St. Joseph Museum

The First Federal Savings and Loan Building, Seventh and Felix, was built in 1889 for the German-American Bank by St. Joseph's leading architectural firm, Eckel & Mann. Their designer was Harvey Ellis, a brilliant draftsman responsible for many buildings in the United States. The building is constructed of both standard and molded brick in smooth and quarry-faced textures with worked sandstone decoration and sculptural detailing. Several of the more notable of these details are the quarry-faced, heavy-cut stone voussoirs of the arches surrounding the main entrances on the north and east sides, the finely tooled pilasters, jambs, and zoomorphic figures on the two major facades, and the finely carved column capitals, mouldings, laurel wreaths, and swags in various locations on the exterior.

First Federal Savings and Loan purchased the bank in 1974 and restored the landmark, making it into a usable modern structure yet retaining its dignity and originality. Work was completed in the fall of 1976, and the building was listed in the National Register of Historic Sites in 1978. Photograph by Don Reynolds; courtesy of the St. Joseph Museum

These pictures of buildings and exhibits are of the new era exposition sponsored in 1889 by St. Joseph businessmen at a cost of $1,000,000. The first steel railway coach is shown left, center, and the Ladies' of Delights at upper left. To the right of it is the grandstand, and the "Reporters Lodge," for the use of newspaper men is directly beneath the grandstand. The wigwam at the bottom was known as "Scouts' Retreat," and the other building was the exhibit of a pioneer railroad, the Chicago, St. Paul, and Kansas City. Photograph courtesy of the St. Joseph News-Press

The Park Bank, Tenth and Penn streets, was established in 1889. It is still doing business at the same location but in 1976 became the United Missouri Bank of St. Joseph. The building has been remodeled several times. Photograph from St. Joseph, Missouri

118

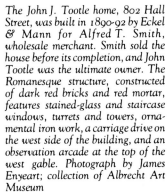

The John J. Tootle home, 802 Hall Street, was built in 1890-92 by Eckel & Mann for Alfred T. Smith, wholesale merchant. Smith sold the house before its completion, and John Tootle was the ultimate owner. The Romanesque structure, constructed of dark red bricks and red mortar, features stained-glass and staircase windows, turrets and towers, ornamental iron work, a carriage drive on the west side of the building, and an observation arcade at the top of the west gable. Photograph by James Enyeart; collection of Albrecht Art Museum

The Josiah Beattie Moss home, 906 Sylvanie Street, was built in 1890-92 by Eckel & Mann. Josiah Moss made his fortune in the lumber, banking, and real estate businesses. Impressed by the style and graceful architecture of the French chalets of the Loire Valley, Moss wanted a unique house with an authentic roof garden. The builders created a "fabled castle of fantastic medievalism," reflecting the Romanesque-Gothic motif and featuring leaded glass windows throughout, solid English oak panels, and ornate hardware. The roof garden quickly became a vine-covered area of beauty and charm.

In 1930, the house was sold to the Knights of Columbus and was used as a combination office and clubhouse. In 1974, it was purchased by Mr. and Mrs. E. C. Barbosa. After extensive remodeling and redecorating, the house was reopened as a restaurant, Barbosa's Castillo. Photograph by James Enyeart; collection of Albrecht Art Museum

119

Watson's Grocery at Twenty-Fourth and Frederick Avenue was a busy place in 1892, for the Frederick Avenue streetcar line ended a short distance east. Many grocery stores of this period played the same part in the early life of St. Joseph that the old "coffee houses" did in eighteenth-century English life. The store was a rendezvous for prominent citizens, who would assemble in the evenings around a huge wood stove and discuss the issues of the day. There were few non-essentials in the stores. The stock usually consisted of potatoes and other vegetables in season, several sides of smoked bacon, green coffee, dried peaches and apples, and a bit of country butter (St. Joseph Museum ic). Photograph courtesy of the St. Joseph News-Press

The M. S. Norman home, 624 North Sixth Street, was built circa 1890. Norman was employed by Brittain Dry Goods Company; later, he formed a partnership with C. W. Noyes to wholesale and later to manufacture shoes—Noyes, Norman Shoe Company. Photograph by James Enyeart; collection of Albrecht Art Museum

Felix Street, looking east from Fifth Street, during the late 1800s. Photograph from St. Joseph and Northwest Missouri

The catalogue of the C. D. Smith Drug Company, vintage 1887, was unearthed from musty files of the firm, according to the St. Joseph News-Press. The catalogue was printed by the old St. Joe Steam Printing Company. An engraving on the front cover depicts the C. D. Smith Drug Company building with the latest things in buggies, horse-drawn trolleys, and gas lamp posts. It places the location at 201 North Third Street.

"Color That Yellow Mustache" reads a full-page advertisement for Mason's Magic Hair Dye. The whiskey distiller advertised that his product was good for "malaria, blood poisoning, and consumption."

The old building was torn down and the drug company moved to its present location, 313 South Third Street, in 1890. Photograph courtesy of the St. Joseph News-Press

The C. D. Smith Drug Company, 313-323 South Third, circa 1927. Photograph from St. Joseph Today

121

Fire Station Number Seven, 1007 North Tenth Street, opened February 15, 1892. The driver is Robert Thorpe; Matthew Herson stands at the front wheel, and Joseph Traynor at the rear wheel. Photograph courtesy of the St. Joseph Fire Department and Strathmann Photography

The entire crew of the Brown Transfer and Storage Company is helping to move boilers in this 1896 photograph. Brown Transfer is one of the oldest businesses in St. Joseph. A. M. Brown started the business in 1863 at 213 South Third Street. When the Missouri Pacific Railroad acquired the building, Brown constructed a new building at 920 South Sixth and moved his business there in 1906. The firm is still located there. Because the building was near the Union Depot where most freight was brought to St. Joseph by rail, they obtained many hauling jobs. In addition to delivering from the depot, Brown's also moved people from place to place. They rented buggies and driving-horses for salesmen to cover the surrounding towns that had no rail service. When business was at its peak, Brown's kept about eighty horses on hand. The pay for their employees was from $1.50 to $2.00 for a day that started at 7 A.M. and ended at 6 P.M. Their storage business was also very successful and was considered one of the largest rental and storage spaces in the country. Photograph courtesy of the Brown Transfer and Storage Company and Strathmann Photography

Fire Station Number Four, Southeast, Fourth and Franklin, opened in November 1893. The driver is William Smith. Left to right, standing: foreman Thomas Lyon, Samuel Tischer, Harve, Keene. Photograph courtesy of the St. Joseph Fire Department and Strathmann Photography

1880-1900

In these 1954 photographs, St. Joseph women model dresses worn in
the city during the 1880-90s.

Upper left: Kitty Fenner, left, and
Sally Chesmore show that walking
up steps was no simple matter in the
sweeping dresses of the past. Kitty
wears an olive silk taffeta trimmed
with yellow ruching and black lace.
Sally's brown moire boasts puffed
sleeves and a bustle-backed skirt.

Center right: Cathy Smith models
a dress that was worn to the Julia
Comstock-Eugene Field wedding
reception. Fashioned of royal blue
taffeta and velvet, the overskirt
billows into a lengthy train. The
diminutive ruffled parasol was an
important accessory to every costume
of this fashion.

Lower left: Mrs. John M. Karle is
photographed in a calling ensemble.
The silk cafe au lait dress is topped
with a fringed black overcape of
bead-encrusted taffeta and heavy net
(St. Joseph News-Press). Photographs by Lewis Shady; courtesy of
the St. Joseph News-Press

In 1897, the Mutual Gas Light
Company and the St. Joseph Gas
and Fuel Company, which had been
established in 1890, became the
property of the St. Joseph Gas Company. In the mid-1920s, the company advertised that it served 10,500
customers through 155 miles of gas
mains. The Gas Service Company
office today is located at Eighth and
Francis streets and serves 27,915
customers. Photograph from St. Joseph Today

The Exchange Building houses the
Stock Yards Bank. The St. Joseph
Stock Yards Bank was chartered in
1898 and began business in the Stock
Yards Exchange building which had
just been completed. Gustavus Swift
had just established a large packing
plant in the area. The bank changed
its name in 1955 to the First St. Joseph Stock Yards Bank, which gave
recognition to its consolidation with
the uptown First State Bank (St. Joseph Museum Graphic). The
Exchange Building housed thirty-two
firms to buy, sell, and handle the
stock that was shipped daily. Photograph from St. Joseph Today

On December 31, 1899, the staff members of the Gazette and Herald gathered outside their building at 813 Edmond Street for a picture-taking session. The man second from the left in the front row was Chris Rutt, who was to become the first managing editor of the St. Joseph News-Press in 1903 and to hold the post until his death in 1936. Photograph courtesy of the St. Joseph News-Press

One of the early streetcars that ran to the stockyards and Lake Contrary. Some of the streetcars were equipped with a fender which was lowered to push stray dogs and cats from in front of the streetcar. The streetcars were operated by electricity which was received from a trolley or small wheel riding on an overhead wire. The steel wheels, riding on tracks, constituted the ground system (St. Joseph News–Press). Photograph courtesy of the St. Joseph Museum

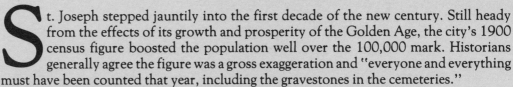

chapter 10
1900-1910

St. Joseph stepped jauntily into the first decade of the new century. Still heady from the effects of its growth and prosperity of the Golden Age, the city's 1900 census figure boosted the population well over the 100,000 mark. Historians generally agree the figure was a gross exaggeration and "everyone and everything must have been counted that year, including the gravestones in the cemeteries."

The industrial growth continued, and there was considerable new building. St. Joseph became the third largest meat-packing center in the world, and the value of packing house products entered into millions of dollars annually. With the packing houses, came additional jobs and an expanded economy. Downtown was developing into an up-to-date metropolitan district with fine stores, hotels, and restaurants, and people were moving from place to place on the newly extended streetcar lines.

St. Joseph has always been a town of fine churches and schools. The first church service was held in Blacksnake Hills in 1838, when a wandering Jesuit priest came to Robidoux's lonely log cabin. A primitive altar was fashioned from a rude table, and mass was celebrated with only Robidoux and a few Indians present. Before churches were built, traveling preachers held services in homes, schoolhouses, and for a time in a log saloon. The first log church in the city was built in 1843 by a Presbyterian minister, Reverend Reeves, at Fourth and Jules. He helped cut the timber for the church, and he and his wife and children lived in a stable while he and his small congregation built the church. Today, St. Joseph has more than 100 churches, many of them of striking beauty.

Private education in the city dates back to 1845, when Mrs. Israel Landis opened a "female seminary"; public education to 1860 when the First, Second, and Third Ward schools were opened. Schools were closed during the Civil War. They were reopened in 1864, and schoolhouse construction has grown rapidly since.

The present jail was constructed in 1909 at a cost of $100,000. A section on the second floor was built for inside hangings: it included a steel trap door, a large eye ring in the ceiling for the rope, and a hanging harness. However, this equipment was never used (*St. Joseph News-Press*).

In a copy of the municipal reports of the city, 1901-02, the Health Department reported it didn't quite know how to cope with the smallpox epidemic which had raged off and on for two years. It also announced it had abolished the post of dog catcher because several persons had been nearly killed in arguments over dogs. Police arrests included five for reckless bicycle riding and six for boys jumping on moving streetcars.

The first edition of the *St. Joseph News and Press*, September 21, 1903, announced that Grace Haywood had taken the Lyceum Theatre by storm and that the Gentry Brothers Famous Animal Show was playing at the showgrounds. The Schlitz Cafe advertised a merchant's lunch for 25¢ to 40¢.

The Wells Fargo & Company Express office at 414 Felix around the turn of the century. Photograph courtesy of the St. Joseph Museum

The history of the Electric Theatre dates back to the turn of the century, at which time there was a skating rink in the building. The rink was later converted to a combination vaudeville and cinema house called the Majestic. In 1931, the business was acquired by the Dubinsky Brothers. Around 1960, the building was reduced in size, allowing for a parking lot in back, and was redecorated for office, store, and restaurant space (St. Joseph News-Press). The building was razed in the 1970s. Photograph from St. Joseph Today

Mr. and Mrs. Mathias Heckel and their five children are shown in the living room of their home around the turn of the century. Heckel was a tinsmith while in Germany and invented the "circular" stove pipe which tended to trap the heat and provide more warmth for the room. Photograph courtesy of George K. Heckel, Jr. and Strathmann Photography

Heckel's Benevolent Home, Second and Michel streets, was established by Mathias Heckel, who came here from Germany in 1881. He was a member of the German Benevolent Society, which had as its object, when first instituted, the extension of aid to German immigrants arriving in St. Joseph. Many of them, in that early day, were unable to express themselves in any but their native language. The Society was organized on the broad basis of human charity and was non-sectarian in its character. Photograph courtesy of George K. Heckel, Jr. and Strathmann Photography

The congregation of the German Lutheran Church met in one of the second-story rooms of the Heckel Benevolent Home. Photograph courtesy of George K. Heckel, Jr. and Strathmann Photography

The First Baptist Church, Thirteenth and Francis streets, was built 1895-1901. Previous to that, the First Baptist Church was a brick structure on the southeast corner of Sixth and Francis streets, built in 1856 (Lilly, History of Buchanan County). Photograph from Rutt, History of Buchanan County

The Christ Episcopal Church at Seventh and Francis streets. The Country Gothic Church was built in 1877, less than a year after the first church at this location burned. It cost $20,000 to construct. It is the oldest Protestant church in continuous use in St. Joseph. It is said that the earliest services of the Christ Church were held in the garden-orchard of Kate Howard on Fifth Street before there was a church. Sometimes curious Indians peered through the bushes and listened to the canticles (St. Joseph Museum Graphic). The present church features Tiffany and German stained-glass windows and an organ brought from Norwalk, Connecticut, in the 1890s, according to an account in the St. Joseph News-Press. Photograph from Rutt, History of Buchanan County

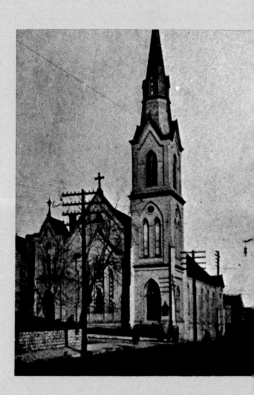

The Tabernacle Congregational Church was built in 1891 at Thirteenth and Jule streets (Rutt, History of Buchanan County). Photograph from Rutt, History of Buchanan County

The First Presbyterian Church was built on the northeast corner of Seventh and Jules streets in 1868 and stood until 1909. In 1908, it was decided to build a new building on the same site. The new building was dedicated on February 12, 1911. Since 1911 the old parsonage to the north of the church has been removed and the building has been extended to Faraon Street. Photograph from Rutt, History of Buchanan County

Street views in St. Joseph during the early part of the century. Photograph from Rutt, History of Buchanan County

According to the St. Joseph News-Press, this was the scene at Third and Edmond streets sometime around the turn of the century. The view is to the north on Third Street. It was a big day at the Apple Market, for wagons were thick at the curb. In the foreground is the John Demond Drug Store; next, George E. Wagner and Company, barbers' supplies; F. C. O'Donoghue, wholesale fruits and produce; Sandusky & Company, wholesale fruits and produce, and Doniphan's candies and produce. Garlich's Drug Store is shown at Third and Felix streets. Courtesy of the Frank Zbierski Collection and Strathmann Photography

This was the delivery system of Western Milk Depot, started in 1878, which later became the Western Dairy and Ice Cream Company. The circa-1900 lineup is on Charles Street, west of Fifth and facing south. Standing, second from right, is August Fenner, who advanced to the presidency and headed the company from 1918 to 1948. When he died in 1953, his son, George Fenner, took charge of the business. In 1968, the dairy was sold to the Hiland Dairy Company. Photograph courtesy of the St. Joseph News-Press

Around the turn of the century, an eastbound Jule Street trolley turns the corner at Eighth and Frederick. The former Hirsch store had not been built yet. From the Nellie Loubey Collection; courtesy of Strathmann Photography

This truck was used by the Blue Valley Creamery Company, Main and Jules, to deliver butter at the beginning of the century. In the 1930s, the company started selling pasteurized milk, buttermilk, cottage cheese, and cream as well as butter. The firm is now part of Beatrice Foods, Main and Jules (Utz, Growth and Development). Photograph courtesy of the St. Joseph News-Press

In 1900, milk was sold from wagons and it was ladled out of big cans at 5¢ per quart. A laborer earned $1.50 per day, and he could buy thirty quarts of milk with his money. "The horses which pulled the wagons soon learned the routes and knew where to stop. The truck industry has never been able to come up with anything to duplicate this" (St. Joseph News-Press). Photograph courtesy of the St. Joseph News-Press

"There wasn't much vehicular traffic in the good old days but what there was could sometimes be snarled up, as shown by this picture. The view is up Frederick Avenue from Eighth Street about the turn of the century. A team of horses pulling a wagon has blocked progress of an inbound streetcar, and there was probably much clanging of the bell as the motorman impatiently tried to get his load of nickel-paying customers to the downtown. One of the horses at the delivery wagon parked at the curb has turned to see what the commotion is all about. The tall building at the right is the Irish-American building, one of many structures razed to make room for the Civic Center. This photograph was made by the late David W. Luchsinger in the early 1900s. The glass photographic plate from which the print was made was found in a pile of rubbish behind the former Luchsinger residence at 1024 North Eighteenth Street" (St. Joseph News-Press). Photograph courtesy of the St. Joseph News-Press

The Sheridan-Clayton Paper Company was originally established in 1886 by the Beaumont-Sheridan Paper and Printing Company. This firm was succeeded by the Ashton-Sheridan Company, and the Sheridan-Clayton Paper Company succeeded to the business in 1888. The firm occupied a five-story brick building at 217 and 219 South Second Street (Pictorial St. Joseph). The firm is located at 302 South Third Street today. It moved to this location in 1901. Photograph from St. Joseph Today

Public Library, St. Joseph, Mo.

"Black Maria" was the name of the police patrol wagon which the city bought in 1900 to replace the less handsome rig which police had previously used. There was little privacy, and the men who were hauled to the police station were subject to the stares of bystanders. South St. Joseph was taken into the city that year, and since there were no paved connections with that area, police soon began to complain about taking their handsome wagon into the mud, according to the St. Joseph News-Press. The police judge was prevailed upon to add a dollar to the fine of every drunk hauled from South St. Joseph to police court. The money was used to pay for washing the paddy wagon. Photograph courtesy of the St. Joseph News-Press

The Central Public Library, Tenth and Felix streets, was opened March 13, 1902. Purd B. Wright, a city clerk, led a drive for an election for a library tax in 1890. Voters approved the proposal by a margin of six to one. The library was housed at various locations until it moved into its present building in 1902. The building was built by the school district and has the library on the first floor and school administration offices on the second floor. An important part of the library system is the reference room at Central Library, which houses a treasure trove of historic material. From the Lillian O'Connor Collection; courtesy of Strathmann Photography

134

The King Hill Baptist Church was built in 1902 with an education wing added in 1954. It is located at 5708 King Hill Avenue. Photograph by Wesley Hazelwood; courtesy of Ziph Photography

The Hirsch Brothers Dry Goods Store, Eighth and Felix streets, opened for business October 1, 1903. Reportedly, there was formerly a creek running through the property on which the building now stands. When the building was excavated, the earth was so saturated with water that an extensive canal system was installed to carry off the spring water, and the foundation was built with plenty of cement to properly hold up the pillars that supported the basement, first, and second floors (Utz, *Growth and Development*). Hirsch Department Store did business at the same location until 1965, when the business was moved to the East Hills Shopping Center. The building is now vacant. Photograph from *St. Joseph Today*

An interior view of the Hirsch Brothers Dry Goods Company: on the right side are a soda fountain and several small, round tables at which customers are enjoying what appear to be ice cream sodas. Photograph courtesy of Mary Lee Doherty

Entrance to Krug Park, off St. Joseph Avenue. William Krug and Henry Krug, Sr., operated a packing business at Fourth and Monterey streets, and in 1876 the firm was incorporated as the Henry Krug Packing Company. In the late 1800s, the Krug Brothers gave the initial forty acres of Krug Park to the city of St. Joseph. Henry Krug, Jr., later became manager of the company, and in 1928, he donated nine more acres to the Krug Park area. Later, he gave the city 100 additional acres descending from the hilltop down to the famed Roy's Branch (Boder, St. Joseph Museum Graphic). The wide variety of trees and shrubs, the unsurpassed Bowl, the beautiful drive, and the spacious picnic grounds made Krug Park one of the most attractive parks anywhere. The elaborate plantings, the greenhouse, the children's circus and the other once-familiar features of the park have been gone for years. The park is now undergoing renovation with funds obtained from the Urban Park and Recreation Recovery Agency, Heritage and Conservation Service of the federal government and funds supplied by the Bode Trust Fund of St. Joseph. Photograph courtesy of the St. Joseph Museum

More views of Krug Park. Upper left: Krug Park Theatorium. Upper right: Artesian well. Bottom left: Krug Park flower beds. Bottom right: Krug Park Pavilion. Photograph from Travelers' Souvenir Illustrated, souvenir booklet of the United Commercial Travelers of America

Krug Park during the early 1900s. Photograph courtesy of the St. Joseph Museum

KRUG PARK—THEATORIUM

ARTESIAN WELL

Children's Circus at Krug Park during the early 1900s. Photograph from St. Joseph Today

Solid rubber tires were the "in" thing when D. H. Schmidt Carriage Works built this truck for H. H. Libbe & Co. The truck had an enclosed cab for the driver, and the sides of the truck body were designed to keep the flour dry (St. Joseph News-Press). Photograph courtesy of the St. Joseph News-Press

This photo from the St. Joseph Fire Department is dated 1905, but no identification of the firemen is given. Notice the lantern held by one of the men. The sturdy horses were carefully selected for endurance and intelligence. They needed great strength to pull the heavy equipment over uneven streets and up and down St. Joseph's hills. Photograph courtesy of the St. Joseph Fire Department and Strathmann Photography

A horse pauses for a drink at a public "horse fountain" at Tenth and Lafayette streets. The fountain was drilled and erected in 1905 by the Humane Society. Later, when automobiles became more common, the fountain had to be removed because too many cars were colliding with it in the center of the street. Photograph courtesy of the Buchanan County Historical Society

MISSOURI AND KANSAS
❧ TELEPHONE CO. ❧

TELEPHONE BUILDING
M. & K. Telephone Company, Owners

THE SWITCHBOARD IN OPERATION

CABLE TERMINAL ROOM IN BASEMENT

TELEPHONE BUILDING:

114 South Seventh Street....

ST. JOSEPH, MO.

The Missouri and Kansas Telephone Company built the city's first fireproof telephone exchange building at 114 South Seventh Street and installed an up-to-date switchboard in 1893. From 1907 to 1912, the Missouri and Kansas Telephone Company became an affiliate of the Bell Telephone Company. In subsequent years, Missouri and Kansas again changed nameplates, with the Southwestern Bell Telephone Company taking the billing (St. Joseph News-Press). Photograph from Illustrated Review

In 1906, St. Joseph's Auditorium, 400 North Fourth Street, was built by public subscription. It has a seating capacity of 6,000 and has been the scene of conventions, fairs, and recitals by some of the world's most famous artists. Replaced by the new Civic Arena in 1980, it is now standing idle. Photograph from St. Joseph Today

Organized on a permanent basis in 1844, Francis Street United Methodist Church moved into this structure at Twelfth and Francis in 1905. Prior to that, the congregation had been housed temporarily on Main Street, at Third and Francis and at Seventh and Francis (Lilly, History of Buchanan County). The Gothic building is constructed of Indiana limestone and contains two of the largest stained-glass windows in the area. Photograph by Wesley Hazelwood; courtesy of Ziph Photography

139

This is the St. Joseph Hospital in 1908. The Sisters of St. Vincent de Paul (Sisters of Charity) moved to quarters here in 1883. Joseph Corby donated the block of ground on Powell Street between Ninth and Tenth; the building has been enlarged several times. A new St. Joseph Hospital is in the process of being erected in the east side of the city. Courtesy of the Frank Zbierski Collection and Strathmann Photography

The lobby of the Hotel Robidoux soon after it was built. Courtesy of the Buchanan County Historical Society

The Hotel Robidoux, Fifth and Francis, was opened for business in 1908. Photograph courtesy of the St. Joseph Museum

Colonel Joseph A. Corby erected the Corby (now Corby-Forsee) office building, a fireproof steel structure, at Fifth and Felix streets in 1909. Colonel Corby also built the Bell Telephone Exchange in 1879, and in 1881 he built to Atchison, Kansas, the first telephone line to connect any two cities in the United States west of Buffalo, New York. He also was a pioneer in establishing telegraph lines out to St. Joseph (Boder, St. Joseph Museum Graphic). Courtesy of the Frank Zbierski Collection and Strathmann Photography

This photo is from a picture postal card. In 1908, the St. Joseph Elks Club built this structure on the east side of North Fifth Street, north of Francis Street. In 1935, the Elks sold the building to the Chamber of Commerce, which used the building until the 1960s, when it was torn down to make way for a drive-in facility for the American National Bank. The Elks were organized in 1886 and had offices in the Tootle Theatre building until 1908. In 1935, the Elks moved to the Robidoux Hotel. When the Robidoux was demolished in 1976, the Elks moved to their present location at Tenth and Sylvanie. From the Lillian O'Connor Collection; courtesy of Strathmann Photography

The Bareback Squad exhibits at the "largest military tournament ever held in the United States"—held in South St. Joseph in 1908. During the week of September 21-26, the city was host to 5,000 soldiers, including more than 2,200 mounted soldiers from the Second, Seventh, and Thirteenth Cavalry. In addition to the spectacular exhibitions, contests, and parades, the newly constructed St. Joseph auditorium was opened to the public for the first time when an elaborate military ball took place there the night of September 22. Although the St. Joseph City Directory of 1908 listed twenty-eight hotels in the city, (not counting the brand new Hotel Robidoux which had opened less than a week before the tournament), the city could not provide public accommodations for the estimated number of between 50,000 and 60,000 arena spectators during the week. Several civic-minded families opened their homes to provide inexpensive lodging for the visitors (Mary Lee Doherty, St. Joseph Magazine). Photograph courtesy of Mary Lee Doherty

Main building of the Wyeth Hardware and Manufacturing Company's fireproof structure, seven and
one-half stories, six and one-half
acres floor space, circa 1927. The
buildling at Second and Jules was
built in 1909, and the company has
been located there since 1911.
Photograph from St. Joseph Today

The A. J. Gross Grocery Store, 911
North Second Street, 1909. This
grocery store opened for business in
the 1880s and was operated by
members of the Gross family until
1942. The building was demolished
in 1980. From left to right: Eliza-
beth Vosteen Gross; son, Matthew
Gross; and A. J. Gross. Photograph
courtesy of Virginia Buck and the
St. Joseph Museum

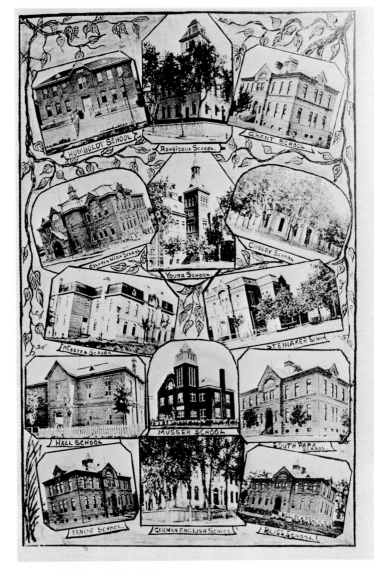

St Joseph schools around the turn of the century.

(1) Humboldt School, Second and Cherry, built 1860, rebuilt on same site, 1907, still in use.

(2) Robidoux School, Tenth and Edmond, opened 1866 as a high school, remodeled in 1895 for a grammar school.

(3) Grant School, Eleventh, near Pendleton Street, built 1895.

(4) Colored High School, Eighteenth and Angelique, built 1888.

(5) Young School, Ninth and Mary, built 1889.

(6) Crosby School, Savannah Avenue and Richardson Street, built 1880.

(7) Webster School, Eighteenth and Highly streets, built 1869.

(8) Steinaker School, Second and Louis, built 1883.

(9) Hall School, Twenty-Sixth and Duncan, built 1887.

(10) Musser School, Twenty-Fourth and Olive streets, built 1894.

(11) South Park School, Seventeenth and Belle streets, built 1888.

(12) Ernst School, Fifth Avenue and St. Joseph Avenue, built 1891.

(13) German-English School, Tenth and Felix, built 1871.

(14) Bliss School, Thirtieth and Olive, built 1890.
Photograph from Views of St. Joseph Today, 1897

This building was constructed in 1910 to house Miss West's School at 2618 Jules Street. The ground floor was used as a dining room for boarding pupils. The top floor was for parties and dancing lessons. All grades were taught, from kindergarten through high school. Elaborate commencement exercises were held, some at the Prinz's Dancing Academy, Tenth and Robidoux Streets. Photograph courtesy of Pictorial St. Joseph

Swift and Company's Prize Six
Horse Draft Team exhibited at
Interstate Live Stock and Horse
Show, September 25-30, 1911.
Photograph courtesy of the Buchan-
an County Historical Society

chapter 11

1910-1920

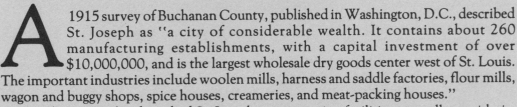

A 1915 survey of Buchanan County, published in Washington, D.C., described St. Joseph as "a city of considerable wealth. It contains about 260 manufacturing establishments, with a capital investment of over $10,000,000, and is the largest wholesale dry goods center west of St. Louis. The important industries include woolen mills, harness and saddle factories, flour mills, wagon and buggy shops, spice houses, creameries, and meat-packing houses."

The report also described St. Joseph transportation facilities as excellent, with six railroads serving the city, one terminal and two interurbans. "Improved rock and gravel roads lead into St. Joseph and dirt roads are in good condition although they wash badly. The public school system of the county is recognized as one of the best in the state. All parts of the county are supplied with rural mail delivery and the telephone is in general use."

The 1910 census had shown St. Joseph with 77,403 residents which is pretty close to the present population.

World War I began July 28, 1914. American manufacturers and farmers found the Allied Nations eager to buy their products, and local prices advanced. By the use of submarines the Germans tried to cut off the flow of supplies. American ships were sunk; lives and property were lost. On April 6, 1917, the United States declared war on Germany. Soon the slogans "Make the world safe for democracy" and "A war to end war" were on everyone's lips. St. Joseph, with the rest of the nation, learned about "nuisance taxes" on such things as theatre and railroad tickets, telephone and telegraph messages, club dues, and many other "luxuries." Postage for a letter was raised from two cents to three. Shortages and rationing had to be coped with.

Fortunately, this country's involvement in the conflict was short, and the number of local casualties was small. The Armistice was signed November 11, 1918. Edwin R. McDonald, writing in the *St. Joseph News-Press*, describes his memories of the day: "'St. Joseph Goes Wild,' shouted a *News-Press* headline. Mayor J. C. Whitsell declared Armistice Day a holiday with all business houses closed, but well before the general public knew about it, employees simply walked out. Workmen threw down tools, brought flags and fireworks and formed impromptu parades. . .Marchers, moving four abreast, entered stores on Felix, Edmond and Francis, tramped through the aisles and left, followed by clerks. Until noon congestion was so great in the streets no ordinary traffic was moving."

President Wilson issued a proclamation: "Everything for which America has fought has been accomplished."

Witt's Neighborhood Bakery, 1802 St. Joseph Avenue. This picture was taken in 1911 when the neighborhood bakery and confectionery store was a common sight. Bernard Witt, Jr., is the small boy in the picture. His sister Marie, now Mrs. Harry Sauer, holds the hand of their father, Bernard Witt. Others pictured are Margareta Witt and Anna Meyer. Photograph courtesy of the St. Joseph News–Press

In 1912, the St. Joseph Fire Department purchased a Velie Touring Car, the first piece of motorized equipment for the department. Hank Bassing is the driver. Photograph courtesy of the St. Joseph Fire Department and Strathmann Photography

The City Workhouse, 913 North Third. For around sixty years, many persons convicted in police court in St. Joseph and unable to pay fines were ordered to the city workhouse to work out their fines. They worked on a rock pile in the yard adjoining the building or worked on city streets (St. Joseph News–Press). The workhouse remained in use until the early 1920s. Photograph courtesy of the St. Joseph News–Press

The monument across Penn Street from the Pony Express Stables in Patee Park in St. Joseph. Present at the dedication, April 3, 1913, were Buffalo Bill Cody, right, and former Pony Express rider Charlie Cliff, left. (St. Joseph Museum Graphic). Photograph courtesy of the St. Joseph Museum

This view shows part of the crowd present when Buffalo Bill and Charlie Cliff dedicated the monument in Patee Park marking the place where the first Pony Express started. Photograph courtesy of the St. Joseph Museum

This is a night-time view of the "City Worthwhile" sign which was activated each evening by an employee of the St. Joseph Power and Light Company who also manually turned on the other electric advertising displays in the downtown area of the city. The sign was in existence some twenty years (Drannan, St. Joseph News–Press). In the 1920s, St. Joseph was known as the "city of bright lights as soon as the sun goes down" and was rated first place in the Midwest for brilliance of business thoroughfares. The sign was removed in the 1930s. Max Habecker photograph; courtesy of the St. Joseph Museum Collection

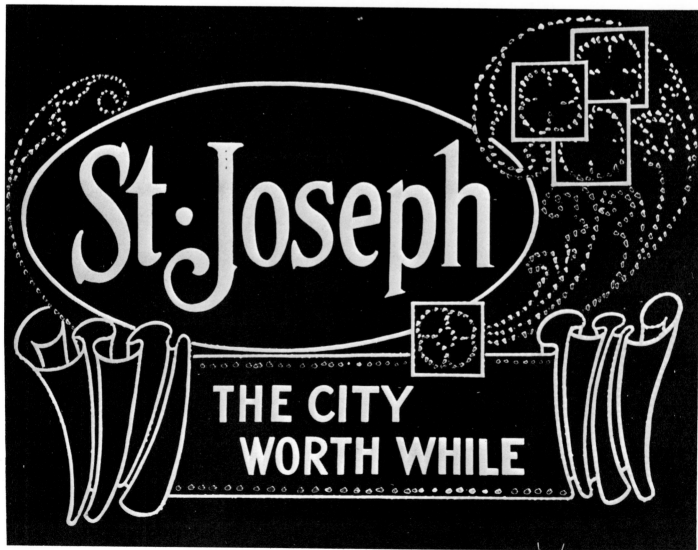

This photograph is a daytime view of the sign, "St. Joseph, The City Worthwhile," atop the Corby Building, Fifth and Felix streets. According to Walt Drannan (St Joseph News-Press), the sign, erected April 1914, was 58 feet wide and 64 feet high, and towered some 218 feet above street level. The letters of the words were 12 feet high, and the sign carried 3,800 incandescent lamps consuming, even in those days, $480 worth of electricity per month. Max Habecker photograph; courtesy of the St. Joseph Museum Collection

The St. Joseph Grain Exchange was founded in 1915, a successor to the St. Joseph Board of Trade. From the time of its inception, it has been located in the Corby Building, Fifth and Felix streets. This photograph shows the St. Joseph Grain Exchange trading floor in 1924. Left to right: Harry Gregory, Charles A. Geiger, Fred Wilkins, Al Muench, C. L. Shaw, Ralph Boyer, Carl Duehren, Duff Taylor, unidentified, Charles Hauber, R. E. Wiese, Henry Fogg, Monty Norton, Gordon Heald, Ed Gumbert, A. Gundelfinger, Fred Watts, and Jack Flynn. Photograph courtesy of the St. Joseph Grain Exchange and Strathmann Photography

Albert H. Bottorff of St. Joseph served in the U.S. Army during World War I, 1917-1918. Photograph courtesy of James Bloom

Central High School, Missouri Western's first home. Missouri Western State College first put down "roots" in 1915 with thirty-five students in the old Central High School at 809 South Thirteenth Street. In that building, junior college and high school students moved together from class to class while the junior college was part of the St. Joseph school district. Today the site is the location of the Naval Reserve Training Center. St. Joseph Junior College was one of only eight in the nation in 1915. Photograph courtesy of Missouri Western State College, The Griffon

Flag display near the court house in June 1916. American patriotic fever was at a high point that year although the United States had not yet entered World War I. One of the big events of that year was a Preparedness Day parade, according to the St. Joseph News–Press. All businesses and factories were closed, and one of the largest parades in the history of the city was held. A feature of that parade was the large American flag carried by the men in the picture. The late Edward Watters, fifth from the right at the lower section, was one of those holding the flag when it was displayed. Photograph courtesy of Mrs. Grace Watters

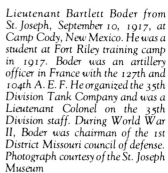

Lieutenant Bartlett Boder from St. Joseph, September 10, 1917, at Camp Cody, New Mexico. He was a student at Fort Riley training camp in 1917. Boder was an artillery officer in France with the 127th and 104th A. E. F. He organized the 35th Division Tank Company and was a Lieutenant Colonel on the 35th Division staff. During World War II, Boder was chairman of the 1st District Missouri council of defense. Photograph courtesy of the St. Joseph Museum

This was the scene on April 22, 1917, when at the height of World War I fever a huge American flag, thirty by fifty feet, was raised atop King Hill. The St. Joseph News-Press described the event: "It is estimated that 10,000 persons climbed the steep ascent of the historic hill to witness the impressive ceremony attending the raising. Many thousands of others in automobiles, from porches and roofs of houses on grounds of adjacent hills watched the beautiful emblem rise and gracefully unfold from the top of the 100-foot pole." A Fourth Regiment bugler sounded reveille as the flag was raised by a squad of Marines from the local naval recruiting station, who stood with drawn rifles. A program of patriotic speeches, songs, and music was furnished by the Central High School Band. Photograph from a glass negative owned by Mrs. Ray Malone; courtesy of the St. Joseph News-Press

The parade of the 135th Infantry Division upon their return home from World War I. The scene is at Eighth and Felix streets, looking south. Photograph courtesy of Kenneth Bottorff

151

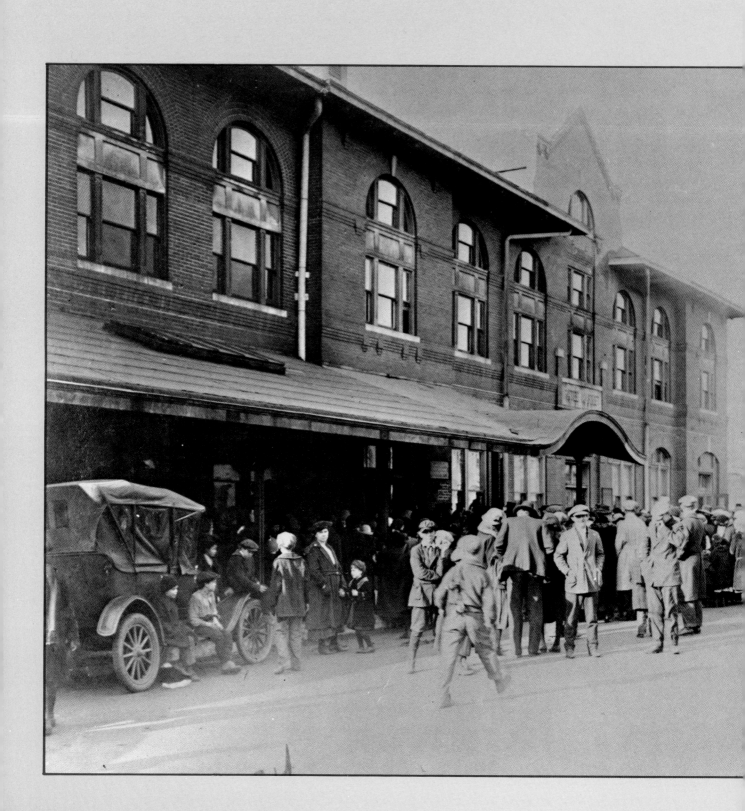

chapter 12

1920-1930

If the "Roaring Twenties" didn't come in with a roar in St. Joseph, they came in with a mighty big bang. The war was over, the boys were home, everything was coming up flappers and sheiks, short hair and short skirts, radios blaring jazz: "Yes, Sir, That's My Baby," the Charleston, and the shimmy were in full swing. New streets were being paved; Model T's, Stanley Steamers, and Pierce Arrows were zipping the more fortunate ones at incredible speeds around St. Joseph and to points beyond.

The second decade of the century was one of great change in the appearance of St. Joseph. A number of new homes and downtown buildings were built. Along with the "City Beautiful" movement, the park board engaged the services of Jacques Greber, an internationally famous landscape gardener of Paris, France, to come to St. Joseph to make ground plans for the Civic Center and the boulevard system. The land was bought, the new City Hall was built, and the grounds were beautified. A $1,904,000 bond issue passed in 1926 to establish a park and parkway system.

In 1927, the spectacular Missouri Theatre was opened. While not the first of St. Joseph's many theatres, it was, by far, the most elaborately ornamented structure in the city, featuring the so-called "Hollywood–Oriental" design.

The adjoining business block was constructed as soon as the theatre was finished, in compatible design style. When this building opened, the second floor was the location of the Prinz Dancing Academy. Edward Prinz, proprietor of the Academy, was the father of Leroy Prinz, of Hollywood fame. Prinz later moved his academy to another location, but this area was the location of a dance studio for many years. Across the street, the Electric Theatre was built.

This quote from Ben Hall's The Best Remaining Seats, aptly portrays the importance of the theatre on the cultural and social life of this era: "The Twenties were a time of extremes...extremes of wealth, poverty, culture....People were stirred like lemmings, to 'go places and do things.' And so they went to the movies, religiously, once a week. Here at last was Aladdin's arc-lit lamp. Here was the chocolate-coated lotus flower, the air-conditioned castle in Spain, the ageless Sirens accompanied by the mighty Wurlitzer—and all for 25 cents (before 6 o'clock)."

Things looked bright and the future held great promise for most of the decade. Then in 1929 came "Black Monday," the Stock Market crash, and the subsequent Great Depression that again brought St. Joseph to an economic crisis.

A crowd gathers at Patee Market, Tenth and Lafayette, in the early 1920s. The occasion that caused the crowd to collect cannot be determined. Patee Market was built by John Patee in 1858 and underwent extensive remodeling in 1907. Today, the building houses a Public Health Clinic. Photograph from the Max Habecker album; courtesy of the St. Joseph Museum

Edmond Street scene in the early 1920s. The St. Joseph News–Press building can be seen at the extreme right of the picture. Photograph courtesy of the Buchanan County Historical Society

This is a view of Fifth Street in the early 1920s. Looking south, at the left, is the former Dr. A. V. Banes building. At the extreme right is the old Lyceum Theatre. Next to it is the Robidoux Hotel. The building with the flag is the Corby Building, Fifth and Felix. The Lyceum, which was converted to a garage, and the Robidoux have been demolished to make way for a new bank and office complex. From the Lillian O'Connor Collection; courtesy of Strathmann Photography

This is believed to be one of the earliest airplanes to land in St. Joseph (in the early 1920s). From the Nellie Loubey Collection; courtesy of Strathmann Photography

The first re-run of the Pony Express of 1860-61 was made in 1923. Robert Lee Shepherd, twenty-five-year-old Pony Express rider of 1923, received a handshake from Mayor George E. McIninch, dressed as Mayor Jeff Thompson was in 1860 when he officiated at the first Pony Express departure. The man at left is Charles Waddles, president of the Chamber of Commerce in 1923. At 10:01 A.M., President Calvin Coolidge in Washington, D.C., pressed a gold key. A gong sounded here, the signal for the rider to dash from the Pony Express Stables on Penn Street on his bay mare, Beauty, to begin the re-run. The object was to beat the best time of the original Pony Express—which was seven days and seventeen hours, St. Joseph to Sacramento. Seventy-five couriers took part in the re-run, and when it ended the time was declared to be approximately forty-two hours faster than the Pony Express record. Photograph courtesy of the St. Joseph Museum and Mrs. T. J. Sherman

The St. Joseph Junior College's Girls' Basketball Team in 1922. Photograph courtesy of Missouri Western State College. The Griffon

Prairie schooner pulled by oxen at the 1923 Pony Express re-run. Prairie schooners and other Civil War trappings were assembled for the pageant, which opened Monday night, August 26, at Lake Contrary and ran through the following Saturday night. Before each performance there were afternoon and evening attractions; circus acts, vaudeville, fireworks, contests, concerts by McNutt's Band appearing as the Rosenblatt Band, and musical numbers. At that time, Rosecrans Field was adjacent to Lake Contrary, and both army and civilian aircraft were on display there. Walter Beach, who would later develop the Beachcraft plant in the city, was also present (St Joseph News-Press). Photograph from the Nellie Loubey Collection; courtesy of Strathmann Photography

155

Part of the St. Joseph Junior College freshman class in 1924. Photograph courtesy of Missouri Western State College, The Griffon

Men and women in the Pony Express Re-run Parade are dressed in attire of 1860. In the picture is Charlie Cliff, a real Pony Express rider. He had carried the mail from January 1861 until the service stopped the following September. Photograph from the Max Habecker album; courtesy of the St. Joseph Museum

Lake Contrary had lotus lillies and a Lotus Club, a landmark for many years. The building was about two blocks north and west of the park and the amusement section. At one time it could be reached by streetcar. Persons fond of good food thought nothing of spending as much as a dollar for a fine meal there. Fire destroyed the club in 1923, and it was not rebuilt. From the Nellie Loubey Collection; courtesy of Strathmann Photography

Shoot the Chutes, Lake Contrary Park. The amusement park was the lake's most popular attraction. Shoot the Chutes featured a boat pulled by chains to the top of a tower, then turned and released to slide on greased skids into the Midway Lagoon. There were also the penny arcade, shooting gallery, skating rink, Giant Dipper, and the Old Mill, among other festivities. Although the park was sold and closed in 1964, the lake is still a favorite spot for swimming, boating, and fishing. Photograph courtesy of the Buchanan County Historical Society

Shoot the Chutes, Lake Contrary Park, St. Joseph, Mo.

1920-1930

St. Joseph's municipal airport, Rosecrans Field, located just northwest of the city, was dedicated September 30, 1925.

Upper left: Travelair plane and Truman Wadlow (in flying suit), Travelair representative at St. Joseph.

Upper right: Mail planes and employees of N. A. T. shop at Rosecrans Field.

Center left: The huge beacon light on Wyeth hill that lights the night flyer's way to Rosecrans Field. It can be seen 120 miles away.

Center right: Floodlight at Rosecrans Field. When all five are on, a newspaper can be read a mile away.

Bottom left: Municipal Hangar at Rosecrans Field.

Bottom right: Two Birdwing planes, manufactured in St. Joseph.

In the early 1930s, the airport was moved directly west in the French Bottoms area where it is presently located. Photograph from St. Joseph Today

The Country Club Saloon was a popular place on what was evidently a warm day (time and place not identified). After Prohibition came and went, drink places were not saloons but taverns. Photograph courtesy of the St. Joseph News–Press

1. Travelair plane and Truman Wadlow (in flying suit), Travelair representative at St. Joseph.
2. Mail planes and employees of N. A. T. shops at Rosecrans field, St. Joseph's fine airport.
3. The huge beacon light on Wyeth hill that lights the night flyer's way to Rosecrans field. It can be seen 120 miles away.
4. Flood light at Rosecrans field. When all five are on, a newspaper can be read by their light a mile away.
5. Municipal Hangar at Rosecrans field.
6. Two Birdwing planes, manufactured in St. Joseph.

St. Joseph Hospital, Tenth and Powell, in the 1920s. The original building had undergone remodeling and expansion. The Daughters of Charity operated the hospital until the spring of 1974 when another group in the community took over the control. Photograph from the Lillian O'Connor Collection; courtesy of Strathmann Photography

St. Joseph Junior College's Boys' Basketball Team in 1925.
  Left to right, back row: Sawyers, Craig, Coach Creek, Kendall, Saunders, Yates. Front row: Bradley, Birmingham, Welch, Carr, Kapp, Hinkle.
  "The group of J.C. Warriors taken the night before they took Conception to a trouncing; score, 59 to 23. In the picture they look harmless, but put a basketball in their hands and give them a basket to shoot at and they suddenly develop into a group of which a 'Mama' wildcat would be proud (The Griffon). Photograph courtesy of Missouri Western State College, The Griffon

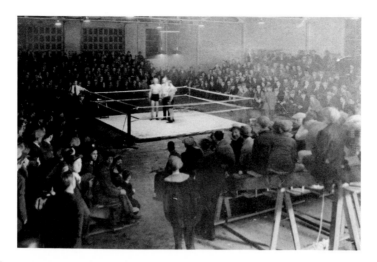

Amateur boxing matches were held at the St. Joseph Light and Power Company's north car barns on St. Joseph Avenue where company horses (during the late 1800s), then streetcars, then trollies, then buses were parked and serviced. The multi-windowed doors lead onto St. Joseph Avenue. The matches were held during the 1920s and 1930s. The public was invited and obviously attended. Photograph courtesy of the St. Joseph Light and Power Company and Strathmann Photography

Four colonels of the Missouri National Guard are in St. Joseph. From left to right: Colonel John D. McNeely, Colonel W. E. Stringfellow, Colonel Charles A. Lindbergh, and Colonel Joseph A. Corby. The photograph was taken at the St. Joseph air field at the time Lindbergh was making a good-will tour of seventy-five American cities in the interest of aviation during the 1920s (St. Joseph Museum Graphic). Photograph by Don Reynolds; courtesy of the St. Joseph Museum

The Everett school building at Fourteenth and Olive. St. Joseph Junior College moved to this building in 1925. Photograph courtesy of Missouri Western State College, The Griffon

Looking west on Felix Street from a point just east of Frederick in the 1920s, one sees a traffic officer in the Eighth Street intersection and a mingling of horse-drawn and motor vehicles. In the foreground, a boy in knickers stands on a brick street. At right: Schroers Drug Store, Kirkpatrick Jewelry Company, Bell Catering Company, and Jenkins Music Company. At left: Bernard Newburger's Millinery, Bass Brothers Dentists. The lettering above the Seventh Street intersection advertises the Colonial Theatre at 111 North Seventh (St. Joseph News-Press). Photograph courtesy of the St. Joseph News-Press

The second Einbender store was located at Tenth and Sacramento in the early 1920s. The first Einbender store was a grocery store, opened in 1919 at Tenth and Corby. Sylvia Einbender added a rack of uniforms on the balcony of the store and over the years managed to make it grow into a multi-million-dollar fashion empire (Gale Holland, St. Joseph Magazine). "We sold ten dollar dresses to girls working at Western Tablet," Mrs. Einbender explains. "They would come in at lunch time and of evenings and try on the dresses behind the barrels that my husband and I plucked chickens and grain out of." Photograph courtesy of Einbender's

The 1926-27 Archery Club at St. Joseph Junior College. Left to right, back row: Bundy, Petrie, Vera Zimmerman. Front row: Seal, Verna Zimmerman, Miss Gates, Hagen, Jennings. Kneeling: Bowen.
"For the first time in its history, Junior College has a Department of Physical Education for women. It attempts to give college girls an opportunity to participate in wholesome recreative activities. Archery is now being incorporated into the physical education department of the college" (The Griffon). Photograph courtesy of Missouri Western State College, The Griffon

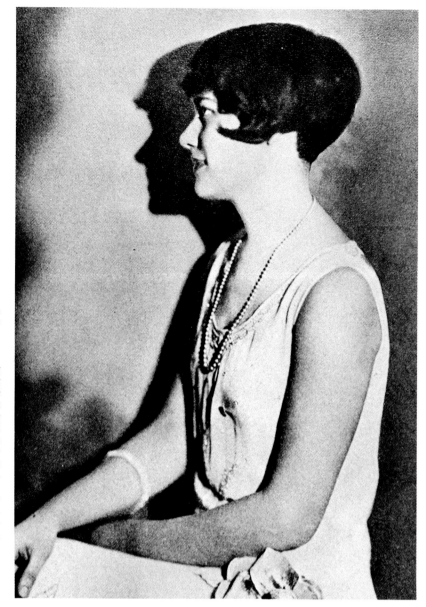

Mabel Byers, "Miss Junior College," 1926-27. Photograph courtesy of Missouri Western State College, The Griffon

St. Joseph stockyards and packing houses, viewed from the top of King Hill. The Missouri River is in the background. By 1927, livestock raising and meat-packing were St. Joseph's largest industries, and the city was the fifth largest livestock market in America; more than four million head of livestock were handled here annually, and twenty-two states contributed to the receipts. In 1912, Armour and Company purchased the Hammond plant, and in 1923, they purchased the Morris and Company plant. Swift and Amour were then the two principal meat-packing plants in St. Joseph. Seitz Packing Company also did a good business. Photograph from St. Joseph Today

William L. Goetz was president of the St. Joseph Museum from its beginning in 1927 until his death in 1953 at the age of eighty-six years.

The Museum had its beginning as a Children's Museum, the brainchild of Orrel Marie Andrews and a group of her St. Joseph Junior College students. As a museum also for adults, it became the pet project and financial problem for Goetz. He purchased the famous Harry L. George American Indian collection for the Museum. By 1942, the Museum had outgrown its three small rooms on the top floor of the Public Library Building and was moved to the A. J. August home on Nineteenth and Felix streets. In 1948 it was moved to its present quarters at Eleventh and Charles streets. Goetz and the Goetz Brewing Company donated $35,000 for the purchase of the building, and Mr. Goetz gave an additional $35,000 for the remodeling and renovating of the building. In 1948, the people of St. Joseph voted with better than a two-thirds majority a mill tax levy of one-half mill on the dollar for the permanent support of the St. Joseph Museum (St. Joseph Museum Graphic). Photograph courtesy of the St. Joseph Museum

Scenes at St. Joseph Country Clubs (1927).
   (1) Clubhouse of St. Joseph Country Club, Ridgeland Road; inset, tree-lined walk leading to clubhouse
   (2) The putting green and clubhouse at the Highlands Golf and Country Club
   (3) The clubhouse at Moila Golf Club.
   A fire later damaged the Country Club Clubhouse, and it was rebuilt along slightly different lines. Photograph from St. Joseph Today

St. Joseph City Hall, Eleventh and Frederick, a structure of Indiana limestone with stately Ionic columns, was dedicated July 7, 1927. The seven-and-a-half acre acquisition and City Hall construction cost nearly $1,700,000. A planned children's theatre and art museum were never completed due to the 1929 recession. Photograph by Don Reynolds; courtesy of the St. Joseph Museum

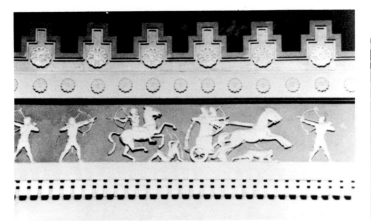

Interior carvings of the Missouri Theatre were done by Waylands Gregory, a student of Lorado Taft. Photograph courtesy of the Performing Arts Association of St. Joseph, Incorporated, and Strathmann Photography

On either side of the stage of the Missouri Theatre were carved figures of the winged bull bearing the head of royal dignitaries. Courtesy of the Performing Arts Association of St. Joseph, Incorporated, and Strathmann Photography

June 25, 1927, was opening night for the Missouri Theatre, 715 Edmond Street, the city's $1,000,000, 1,200-seat "movie palace." The unusual architecture gave a little of the appearance of a Turkish mosque with its buff terra cotta, red and blue enameled tile, and three-bayed facade towering above the street. Patrons paid the twenty-five cents admission fee and stepped into an elegant aura of plush carpeting and period furniture. The canopy-like ceiling appeared to be held in place by ropes attached to the side walls. The interior carvings were copied Persian, Arabian, Assyrian, and Hittite creations. Mayor Louis Stigall gave the welcome, and the crowd was treated to a feature—"Rough House Rosie,"—starring Clara Bow, a newsreel, and music by the "golden-voiced" Wurlitzer. The Missouri became the "in" place to go until the end of World War II when the entertainment industry moved to the eastern edge of the city and television became common. The Missouri was closed in 1970 as a movie house, but the building was kept available as a home for the performing arts. In 1976, Town Hall Center, Incorporated, organized and borrowed enough money for repairs urgently needed to keep the theatre operable.

St. Joseph citizens voted a bond issue of $700,000 in 1977 for the purchase and renovation of the theatre as a city center for the performing arts. At the same time, a bond was passed for the construction of a new civic arena building. The city took possession of the theatre in 1978. Photo courtesy of the Performing Arts Association of St. Joseph, Incorporated

165

Employees of the St. Joseph Railway, Light, Heat and Power Company stand outside the utility's former offices at Fifth and Edmond streets to advertise the "Edison Electric Flat Iron and Paragon Folding Clothes Basket." The picture was taken during the 1920s. Photograph courtesy of the St. Joseph Light and Power Company and Strathmann Photography

Chicago Great Western railroad yards in North St. Joseph and to the right, Maple Leaf Boulevard, a unit of the city's parkway. The railroad yards contained seven and three-tenths miles of tracks and had a capacity of 700 cars (1927).

The Chicago Times in 1886 reported that St. Joseph had eleven railroads and seventy passenger trains each day. In 1911, the St. Joseph Union Passenger Station scheduled 120 daily passenger trains. By the 1930s, trucks began to haul livestock to central markets, and people relied on automobiles and airplanes for traveling. Today, St. Joseph has six trunk lines and no passenger trains. Photograph from St. Joseph Today

A snag boat used to remove snags and debris from the Missouri River, operated by the U. S. Army Corps of Engineers, dated March 26, 1928. Photograph from the Department of the Army, Kansas City District

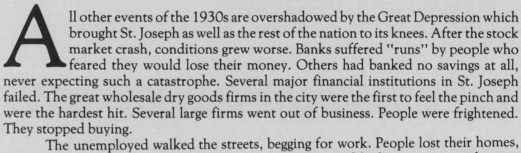

chapter 13
1930-1940

All other events of the 1930s are overshadowed by the Great Depression which brought St. Joseph as well as the rest of the nation to its knees. After the stock market crash, conditions grew worse. Banks suffered "runs" by people who feared they would lose their money. Others had banked no savings at all, never expecting such a catastrophe. Several major financial institutions in St. Joseph failed. The great wholesale dry goods firms in the city were the first to feel the pinch and were the hardest hit. Several large firms went out of business. People were frightened. They stopped buying.

The unemployed walked the streets, begging for work. People lost their homes, cars, even furniture. Many were put out on the street and had to move in with more fortunate relatives. A loaf of bread dropped to five cents, coffee was fourteen cents per pound, steak, fifteen cents, but many could not buy, even at those prices. Transients roamed the streets and mooched or were fed at St. Vincent's Cafe or similar places. Farmers lived in poverty, and many who could not meet the payments on their mortgages had their land taken away from them.

The country was in a desperately serious economic crisis by 1933 when Franklin Roosevelt was inaugurated President and Congress gave him broad powers to "wage war against the emergency." The WPA (Work Projects Administration, a government project that created useful jobs) was one program that brought work to St. Joseph. The city took advantage of the program to move the airport again, this time directly west in the French Bottoms area where it is presently located. WPA labor and money were used to make a longer drive through Krug Park, improving the amphitheatre and constructing Krug Park Lagoon.

Work on the Missouri River provided jobs for hundreds of men who helped to drive piling, to weave willow mats for fighting erosion, and to dump thousands of tons of rock along the river bank to keep the river in its proper channel. Although the WPA provided something like forty dollars per month, the jobs were eagerly sought.

At no time did St. Joseph Junior College better prove its worth than during this era when students could remain at home and for nominal costs obtain an education. The NYA (National Youth Administration) provided job training for unemployed youths and part-time work for needy students at the college. On the honor roll of Junior College students in the fall of 1935, 19 percent were receiving NYA funds, but the entire allotment was only $630 a month. That meant the students were receiving between $10 and $20 per month for from forty to eighty hours of work.

The economy gradually began to improve as the 1940s approached, but the effects of the Great Depression on St. Joseph and the nation were far-reaching and continue to this day.

This photograph is generally thought to show workers making drives through Krug Park during the Depression years. Photograph courtesy of the St. Joseph Museum

The Model T was a popular, and sometimes frustrating, way to get to college in the 1930s. The caption for this picture in The Griffon was simply "Morton, twisting its neck." Photograph courtesy of Missouri Western State College, The Griffon

Circuses used to be presented at Sixth and Atchison streets in St. Joseph during the 1930s and were a popular form of entertainment. Streetcars were a favorite way of getting there. This one still has the fender used to push dogs and cats from in front of the streetcar. Photograph courtesy of the St. Joseph Light and Power Company and Strathmann Photography

One of the buses the St. Joseph Light and Power Company first operated. Note the chassis style. This bus was manufactured and purchased by the company in the early 1930s. Photograph courtesy of the St. Joseph Light and Power Company and Strathmann Photography

Company conductors play checkers in the car barns office area on St. Joseph Avenue. Note the pot-bellied stove and the spittoon. Photograph courtesy of the St. Joseph Light and Power Company and Strathmann Photography

Jerre Ann employees are like one big family and several have been there for thirty or forty years. Left to right, front row: Frances Carolus, Afro Lineberry (who opened the cafeteria in 1930), Hattie Thompson, Jerry Carolus; second row: Geraldine Lawhon, Jean Curry, Jeff Curry; back row: Mary Lou Kephart (ten years of service), Nellie Kerns (twenty-one years of service) and Helen Silvey (eighteen years with the cafeteria). Frances and Jerry Carolus are both over eighty years of age. Photograph courtesy of Geraldine Lawhon

The Jerre Anne Cafeteria, 2640 Mitchell Avenue, opened for business August 2, 1930, on the same corner where it stands today. The grand opening specials included sugar at twenty-nine cents for a five-pound bag and coffee at thirty-five cents a pound. Jerre Anne's thrived even in the Depression years. "We served many a meal for twenty-five cents," says Geraldine Lawhon, one of several family members who keep Jerre Anne's going. "We sold a whole pie for a dime. And we gave away suckers, candy, and ice cream cones to the children. There were so many people out of work, they begged for jobs and willingly worked for ten cents an hour."

In time the family got out of the grocery business and concentrated on the delicatessen and cafeteria, featuring home cooking and home-made pastries. They have enlarged the building and modernized the decor. Photograph courtesy of Geraldine Lawhon

As its enrollment continued to increase, St. Joseph Junior College moved to this building at Tenth and Edmond streets in 1933. The structure had previously been the home of the Robidoux Polytechnic High School. When the college moved to its new campus in 1969, the building at Tenth and Edmond was used to house the artifacts of the Buchanan County Historical Society. Photograph courtesy of Missouri Western State College, The Griffon

Last Electric Car on Streets of St. Joseph.
[News-Press Staff Photographs.]

Mrs. George C. Hax, 401 South Eleventh street, drives her Rau & Lang electric out for the first photographic study in the entire career of the car. It was purchased in 1915 and has served the owner faithfully and without accident ever since. Note the many windows and the generous amount of glass in each. There was no trouble over visibility in an electric. The pneumatic tires are younger than the car, the first tires being solid.

practical by nature, has grown to be something of an electrical engineer in judging the current in a set of batteries; but, even so, she has missed home a time or two by a block. A run-down electric must be towed in; there can be no running up with a gallon of gas to tide it over to the closest filling station.

The only filling station used by an electric is a rectifier which converts commercial alternating current into direct current and charges the storage batteries. There are forty-four batteries in Mrs. Hax's car and the cost per month of recharging them is $4. That represents the fuel bill.

A set of batteries lasts four or five years. Mrs. Hax has bought four sets at a cost of $400 a set.

Operation is Simple.

Tire wear was negligible until the first set of solid tires gave out and that took years. Pneumatic tires are on the car now. The old ones rode smoothly, though, according to Mrs. Hax. Even in the days of rough roads and streets the car ran "like a ..."

Interior of the electric. The long handle is the steering rod. At the left and toward the base of the steering lever is another lever that controls the power. On the dashboard is a clock and a device to open the windshield. The meters below show how much current is being consumed, how much power is left in the batteries and how fast the car is going. ... foot brake

The Albrecht Art Museum, 2818 Frederick Avenue, was built in 1935 by William Albrecht, founder of the Western Tablet Company. The architect was Eugene R. Meier. Georgian in style and standing on four acres, the home was given for an art museum in 1966 by Albrecht's daughter and son-in-law, Mr. and Mrs. W. Conger Beasley. The permanent collection consists of American paintings and drawings. Photograph by James Enyeart; collection of Albrecht Art Museum

This photograph shows the last electric car on the streets of St. Joseph (circa 1938). Mrs. George C. Hax, 401 South Eleventh Street, drove her Rau & Lang electric out for the first photographic study in the entire career of the car. It was purchased in 1915 and served the owner faithfully and without accident. Note the many windows and the generous amount of glass in each. There was no trouble with visibility in an electric. The pneumatic tires were younger than the car, since the first tires were solid.

In the interior view of the electric, the long handle is the steering rod. At the left and toward the base of the steering lever is another lever that controls the power. On the dashboard is a clock and a device to open the windshield. The meters below show how much current is being consumed, how much power is left in the batteries, and how fast the car is going. There were forty-four batteries in the car, and the cost per month of recharging them was $4.00 That represented the entire fuel bill. Mrs. Hax sold the electric car in the 1940s. (St. Joseph News-Press). Photograph courtesy of the St. Joseph News-Press

Construction work along the south bank of the Missouri River downstream of the railroad bridge. Construction was halted due to heavy ice runs, February 20, 1933. Photograph from the Department of the Army, Kansas City District

The old, red-brick police station with
its turret tower at the northeast corner
of Seventh and Messanie was built
the latter part of the nineteenth
century. It served as Central Police
Station until 1939, when the present
station at Ninth and Mary was built.
Scott and Company Canvas Goods
now occupies the building. Photograph courtesy of the St. Joseph
News-Press

Mrs. and Mrs. Albert H. Bottorff,
St. Joseph, in 1935. The auto was a
Model T with an Ames body. A. H.
Bottorff was owner of Farmer's
Equipment Company, Inc., 644
South Sixth Street, from 1932 to
1952. Photograph courtesy of James
Bloom

The first Strathmann Photography
Studio in St. Joseph at 118 South
Eighth Street. The present Strathmann Photography Studio is located
at 3825 Frederick Avenue in East-
ridge Village. Mike Wylie is the
manager. Photograph courtesy of
Strathmann Photography

A. B. Strathmann, shown here, opened the Strathmann Studio, St. Joseph's oldest photographic studio, in 1939. He had had a photographic studio at Atchison, Kansas, since 1929. Strathmann came from a long line of photographers; his father was a photographer who had eleven children, ten of whom became photographers. A. B. Strathmann retired from business in 1962. Photograph courtesy of Strathmann Photography

Central High School, Twenty-six and Edmond streets, facing east, is in the lower center of this photograph, taken in the early 1960s. The building was built in 1932. Photograph courtesy of Mike Wylie and Strathmann Photography

chapter 14

1940-1950

Felix Street, looking west from
Eighth, in the 1940s

Things were just beginning to look bright again for St. Joseph when the Japanese attacked Pearl Harbor. Once more the nation was at war.

Frank Popplewell, professor of history at St. Joseph Junior College, describes the day after that "day of infamy" in *The Fiftieth Anniversary of St. Joseph Junior College:* "Junior College students gathered in the auditorium to hear President Roosevelt call on congress to declare war. There was not a sound, no hysteria, no frenzied clapping—the consensus being now that we are in it, the only sensible thing for us to do is to tighten our belts and fight until victory is ours."

The Junior College faculty had assisted in the first peacetime draft in the history of the nation in 1940, and the war brought the decrease in enrollment that had to be anticipated. Students joined the civil defense movement, and casualty lists gave the first names to be imprinted in bronze and hung on college walls. At the close of 1942, 75 percent of the male students at J. C. were enrolled in the army or navy reserve. Some described the college as "Miss Blum's (after the college dean) Finishing School For Young Ladies." When the bronze plaque honoring the war dead was completed, a total of sixty-one students from the college had made the supreme sacrifice.

The college donated its old lockers and even the stage scenery weights to the scrap metal drive. The Student Senate announced that a War Stamp drive would replace the publication of a yearbook. The town emptied its piggy banks of pennies and nickels as the scarce metals in these coins were needed to replace stored coins.

Everyone was called upon to make sacrifices. Automobile tires were the first commodity to be rationed. Sugar, coffee, canned goods, meats, and butter soon followed. Gasoline was rationed in all parts of the country. "Is This Trip Necessary?" became a familiar slogan. "Blackouts" were held over the city for practice, and people purchasing war bonds were given a free jeep ride through downtown.

The St. Joseph Tank Company of the national guard was activated. Some were sent to Alaska and some to the Philippines. Rosecrans Field was converted to a busy military base, providing pilot training for the Air Transport Command for thousands who trained here before "shipping out" to the war zones.

Military contracts directed civilian industries to make canvas instead of nylons, boots instead of slippers, coffins instead of beds. American flags were also in big demand. Local industries did war work. The Sun Garment Company in the former Patee House completed three contracts manufacturing 1,175,000 army shirts. Walker Manufacturing Company, Eighteenth and Penn, turned out draft regulators for every barracks stove in the United States Army.

When Germany surrendered in 1945 on May 7, Mayor Phil Welch ordered a twenty-four hour ban on the sale of liquor to prevent wild demonstrations of the type which had followed the war's end in 1918. About four months later, when the war ended, St. Joseph really celebrated.

Aerial view of St. Joseph's boulevard system in the 1940s. The plan to connect the existing parks from the northern to the southern boundaries of the city began after World War I. By 1927, the goal was reached, and one can now drive from Krug Park on the north to Hyde Park in the south along a route planned for its beauty. Photograph from New Comers' Key; courtesy of Townsend and Wall

War and Community projects enlisted the active support of Junior College students during the 1940s. Selling war bonds, participating in United Nations Clothing, Red Cross, and Community Chest drives, entertaining at Rosecrans Field, conducting forums and interviews in the interest of world peace, and rolling bandages were some of the projects of the Junior College League of Women Voters. Photograph courtesy of Missouri Western State College, The Griffon

Dancing and bridge at the Junior College Icebreaker, first party of the 1941-42 school year. The Jitterbug dance had hit St. Joseph, but couples were enjoying a slower number in this picture. The graduating class in the spring of 1941—145 graduates— was the largest for the college. Photograph courtesy of Missouri Western State College, The Griffon

Aerial view of St. Joseph's Civic Center in the 1940s. Photograph from New Comers' Key; courtesy of Townsend and Wall

The Goetz Brewery, Sixth and Albemarle, in the 1940s. As the population of the city increased, the demand for beer grew. Goetz enlarged his plant several times and took his sons into the firm. The M. K. Goetz Brewing Company was one of the few breweries that remained in operation during the years of Prohibition. The plant continued to manufacture because the chemists discovered a process of making near-beer—regular beer with the alcohol taken out. It was called Country Club and was in great demand. Goetz Brewing Company was one of St. Joseph's biggest factories during the middle part of the century (Utz, Growth and Development). M. K. Goetz merged with the Pearl Brewing Company in 1960. Pearl phased out of the business in 1975, and some of the buildings were demolished. In 1978, the business was sold to the General Brewing Company of San Francisco. Photograph courtesy of the St. Joseph Museum

Fourth grade pupils at Webster Elementary School, Nineteenth and Highly, make a Junior Red Cross contribution in February 1942. Photograph courtesy of Buchanan County American Red Cross and Strathmann Photography

St. Joseph War Dads helped Red Cross volunteers serve treats for the soldiers who passed through the city at 8:00 P.M. on July 26, 1944. The scene was typical of those re-enacted each evening. Photograph courtesy of the St. Joseph News-Press and Strathmann Photography

At the end of a two-week trip by train and ship from Alaska, these St. Joseph tank company members unpack their barracks bags at Fort Riley, Kansas, April 28, 1944. Photograph courtesy of the St. Joseph News-Press and Strathmann Photography

March 24, 1943; Albert Farris, proprietor of the Modern Lunch in St. Joseph, contributed the entire proceeds of the day to the American Red Cross. Photograph courtesy of the Buchanan County Chapter of American Red Cross and Strathmann Photography

This photograph was taken at the start of the NBC broadcast Monday evening, February 19, 1945, at the St. Joseph auditorium. St. Joseph proved that it really loved Jack Benny: nearly 5,000 people attended each of his two shows. The tickets were given to blood donors of the Red Cross blood bank. Photograph courtesy of the St. Joseph News-Press and Strathmann Photography

A group of Buchanan County Chapter American Red Cross volunteers serves patients on a hospital ship stopping over at Rosecrans Field on February 9, 1945. Photograph courtesy of Buchanan County Chapter American Red Cross and Strathmann Photography

Water Safety Instructor's Course conducted in March 1945 by Eddie Knapp, First Aid Water Safety Accident Prevention (FAWSAP), Field Representative. Photograph courtesy of Buchanan County Chapter American Red Cross and Strathmann Photography

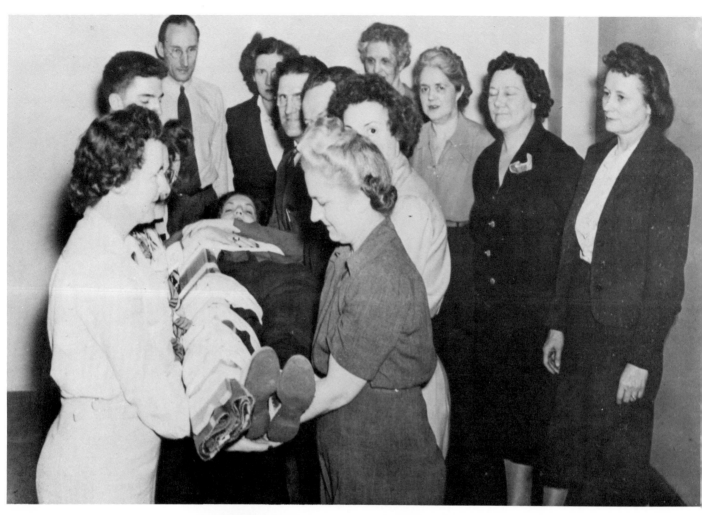

First Aid Instructor's Course conducted in February 1946 by Ernest Vornbrock, FAWSAP Field Representative. Photograph courtesy of Buchanan County Chapter American Red Cross and Strathmann Photography

Mrs. E. E. Wilson, chairman of production for the Buchanan County Chapter of American Red Cross. The mending service mended 518 garments for 344 soldiers. Photograph courtesy of Buchanan County Chapter American Red Cross and Strathmann Photography

56   ST. JOSEPH, MO., NEWS-PRESS, SUNDAY, JULY 1, 1979

ST. JOSEPH NEWS-PRESS EXTRA

WAR ENDS

The last News-Press extra

Mary Ann Forman, Junior College Queen, 1948-49. Photograph courtesy of Missouri Western State College, The Griffon

The last "Extra" printed by the St. Joseph News-Press appeared on Tuesday evening, August 14, 1945. It announced the victory over Japan with a huge headline—"War Ends." Photograph courtesy of the St. Joseph News-Press

Ice jam on the Missouri River, looking downstream, dated February 25, 1949. Photograph from the Department of the Army, Kansas City District

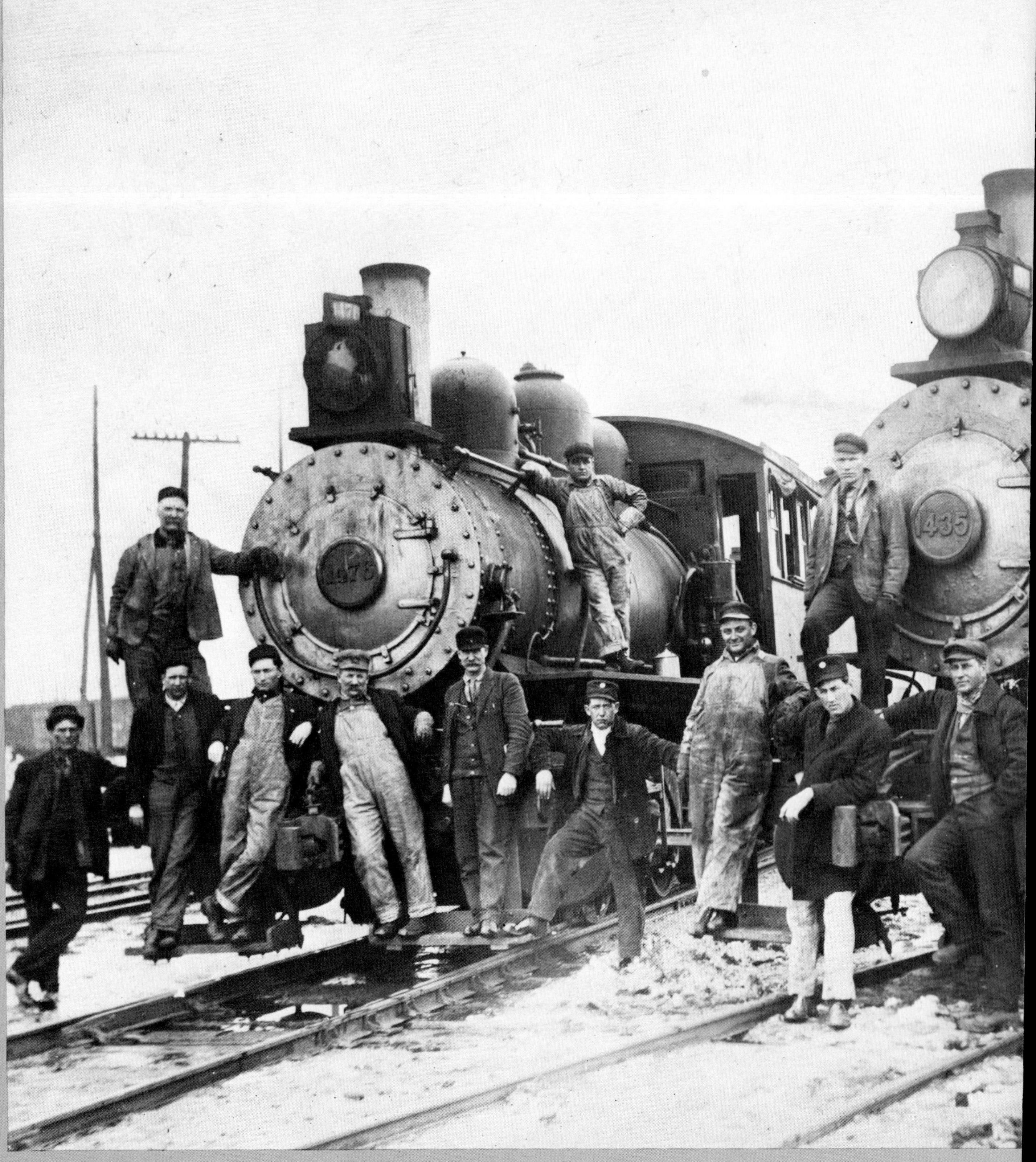
1435

Harry S Truman and daughter Margaret campaign in St. Joseph in October 1948. Photograph courtesy of the St. Joseph Museum

Benton High School, 5655 South Fourth Street, is shown in the lower left of this aerial photograph taken in the early 1960s. The school was built in 1940. Photograph courtesy of Mike Wylie and Strathmann Photography

Rail traffic reigned supreme in St. Joseph until the start of World War I, with hundreds of passenger trains traveling in all directions. Freight was another big business for the railroads. After-the-war slumps in the economy, however, and the advent of the cheap automobile, as well as cheap fuel, started affecting rail travel. The Depression of the 1930s also cut deeply into railroad profits. But when World War II came along, troop trains filled Union Station to the overflow point.

Within a decade after the war, passenger service was in trouble. In 1960, Union Depot was replaced with small stations, and by the late 1960s, all passenger service in St. Joseph was stopped. By the 1970s, remaining railroads in St. Joseph were concentrating on such materials as farm products, automobiles, machinery, and a newly developing role in delivering vast amounts of coal for electrical fuel (St. Joseph News-Press). Photograph courtesy of the St. Joseph Museum

St. Joseph Light and Power Company employees sandbag around the Edmond Street power plant in 1952 when flood waters struck St. Joseph. Photograph courtesy of St. Joseph Light and Power Company and Strathmann Photography

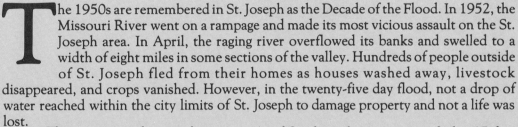

chapter 15
1950-1960

The 1950s are remembered in St. Joseph as the Decade of the Flood. In 1952, the Missouri River went on a rampage and made its most vicious assault on the St. Joseph area. In April, the raging river overflowed its banks and swelled to a width of eight miles in some sections of the valley. Hundreds of people outside of St. Joseph fled from their homes as houses washed away, livestock disappeared, and crops vanished. However, in the twenty-five day flood, not a drop of water reached within the city limits of St. Joseph to damage property and not a life was lost.

The watery nightmare began on April 8 when the river passed the 17-foot theoretical flood stage. The water continued to rise, and Rosecrans Field was evacuated; residents of the valley and the city of Elwood moved to higher ground. On April 22, the water reached 27.2 feet. The next morning the water began to recede, but it was not until May 3 that the river dropped below flood stage.

As the water receded, the full damage came to light. The river had cut a new channel through French Bottoms, separating the city from Rosecrans Field. It had also cut a new channel through the Elwood Bottoms. Highway 36 in the Elwood area was impassable because of the new channel. Two and one-half miles of Union Pacific track were useless. Rosecrans Field runways were covered with tons of silt, and water had reached a height of eight feet inside the airport administration building.

But that same flood proved to be an asset to the St. Joseph area. Up to that time, not much concern had been given to the threat posed by the river. An immediate result of the flood was the investment of millions of dollars in levees, one to protect the St. Joseph industrial area and another to protect Rosecrans Field and the adjacent Kansas area from a repeat of the disaster. The result of the levee construction was the development of flood-free areas on both sides of the river where industries have since spent millions of dollars for new construction. Today, river protection in this area is at a high level, and engineers believe the Missouri River no longer poses a serious flood threat.

Another important event for St. Joseph during this decade took place the day the highest point of the city's skyline came into being—the 750-foot tower for KFEQ-TV at Fortieth and Woodbine Road. The station officially went on the air September 23, 1953, and is one of the oldest television facilities in the state.

Also, the Jet Age arrived at Rosecrans Field in 1958 when the air guard switched to fighter-type planes and later to reconnaissance aircraft. After the war, the army pulled out of the field, but the Missouri Air National Guard has been stationed there since 1947. During 1960, TWA began training their pilots on commercial jet planes at the field. The remaining air traffic is created by general aviation flights.

1950-1960

The Wire Rope Corporation of America is one of St. Joseph's ever-expanding industries, located just to the northwest of the central business district. This aerial view toward the northeast shows the many new structures which have been erected in the left portion of the photograph. Wire Rope offices are housed in the tallest of the white structures at the right. Tracks of the Chicago North-western Railroad bisect the property of the wire rope manufacturing concern. Wire Rope opened for business in St. Joseph in October 1950 and not only fashions wire rope but also fabricates the wire strands used in rope manufacturing. Wire Rope property is bounded on the east by South Fourth Street, on the south by Robidoux and Jule, extends be-yond Antoine on the north, and on the west extends to west of Main Street. Fourth Street is the street at the top of the photograph. Photo-graph courtesy of the Wire Rope Corporation of America

The Missouri River breakthrough on the road on the north side of Lake Contrary, looking west. Floodwaters inundated the area. The 1952 flood spelled the end of the Old Mill—one of its boats rode downstream on the floodwaters as far as Lexington, Missouri. The Shoot The Chutes, weakened by time and heavy water damage, was dismantled soon after. Photograph courtesy of Wesley Hazelwood and Ziph Photography

An employee cuts the grass between two of the reservoirs at the Water Company north of the city on Waterworks Road. All of St. Jo-seph's drinking water comes into this plant from the Missouri River. Photograph courtesy of St. Joseph News-Press and Strathmann Photography

Dredging a new channel for the Missouri River at the St. Joseph Cutoff. Note bank protection and levee construction along the west bank, looking downstream, dated 1952. The April flood of that year resulted from snow-melt and ice conditions generally similar to those of 1943 and 1881. The Omaha stage reached 30.2; the stage was 27.2 at St. Joseph and 30.7 at Kansas City (St. Joseph Museum Graphic). Photograph from the Department of the Army, Kansas City Division

Adlai E. Stevenson, Democratic nominee for President of the United States, campaigns in St. Joseph in 1952 and enjoys a locally grown apple. Photograph courtesy of the St. Joseph Museum

Floods in the Missouri River Basin caused damage of $83 million, Colonel R. W. Love, division engineer at Omaha, estimates. At the same time, Colonel Love notes that flood control structures built on the river since the 1930s have prevented an additional $200 million damage (St. Joseph News-Press). Photograph courtesy of the St. Joseph News-Press

Get Acquainted dance, 1952, at St. Joseph Junior College. The Korean War had come along, and stepped-up military service again had caused the enrollment to tumble. In 1953, the war veterans started returning. Photograph courtesy of Missouri Western State College, The Griffon

Fire Chief Urbansky is pointing to the two old steamers. The Red Bird is in the rear. Chief Urbanski served from December 5, 1927, until January 1, 1952, as chief of the St. Joseph Fire Department. Photograph courtesy of the St. Joseph Fire Department and Strathmann Photography

The new channel of the Missouri River through French Bottoms is shown in the upper portion of this aerial photograph of St. Joseph's central business area in 1956. The body of water at the upper left was what remained of the breakthrough area where the river sloshed through the bottoms in 1952. The white structure in the center of the picture is the Buchanan County Court House. The building in the lower center is the St. Joseph Junior College, and Central Public Library is seen at the right. The view is to the northwest across the central business district (St. Joseph News-Press). Photograph by Dick Jones; courtesy of the St. Joseph News-Press

Air photo section of St. Joseph, 1953, now a city of 80,000 people. The spires of the Immaculate Conception Catholic Church may be seen at the extreme right, center, and directly across to the next to the last building to the left, center, the St. Joseph Junior College, Tenth and Edmond streets. Photograph courtesy of the St. Joseph Museum and Strathmann Photography

Eleanor Roosevelt at Union Passenger Station in 1959 when she visited St. Joseph. Greeting Mrs. Roosevelt are Jane Erickson, a reporter for the News-Press then, and Harold M. Slater, city editor of the paper.

Winter scene in Hyde Park, south
St. Joseph. Photograph courtesy of
Wesley Hazelwood and Ziph Photo-
graphy

chapter 16

1960-1970

St. Joseph Mayor Arthur Meers hands mochila to Lee Shifflett before the Centennial Re-Ride, April 3, 1960. History was re-enacted as the bearded Mayor, wearing stovepipe hat and cutaway coat, portrayed Mayor M. Jeff Thompson of 100 years ago. A cannon was fired from the top of old Patee House to signal the start of the ride. With a slap on the horse's rump, Mayor Meers started the rider on his way amid a tumult of thunderous applause. Over fifty Pony Express Re-run riders from Missouri, Kansas, and Iowa made the ride to Salt Lake City, 1,329 miles distant, in seventy-five hours (Don Reynolds, St. Joseph Museum Graphic). Photograph by Don Reynolds, courtesy of the St. Joseph Museum

St. Joseph had grown and prospered, and life was good here. Perhaps too good because people became too content. They liked their city as it was. As a result, population remained stable for several decades. However, two events in the 1960s brought home the fact that times were changing and that the city must keep in step.

The first crisis that jolted St. Joseph into aggressively seeking new industry was the decision of both Swift and Armour Meat Packing Companies to leave the city in 1967. That meant a loss of 3,000 jobs, or 10 percent of the work force. Facing the situation, business and community leaders alike offered their assistance to help create an industrial development program to attract new industries to replace jobs lost and to avoid similar catastrophes in the future. The Chamber of Commerce came up with a "New Image" campaign— an image of a city which, like the Pony Express rider, was "Changing Horses," acquiring a fresh start for what lay ahead.

A stepped-up program to enlarge and diversify the community's industrial base went into high gear. The intent was to expand and to grow and at the same time to retain the friendly home-town image which the city had known for so long. The first portion of Industrial Park, a 160-acre tract in East St. Joseph, was bought. Whitaker Cable Corporation, Chase and Poe Candy Company, and Stevens Hat Company moved in, soon followed by other firms.

Shopping centers were mushrooming all over the country. In 1965, the East Hills Shopping Center, Frederick and Belt, opened—400,000 square feet of leasable area with free parking space for 28,000 cars. The $4,000,000 building contained ten acres under one roof, a fully enclosed, air-conditioned, heated and landscaped mall with space for thirty shops. Downtown suffered severely. Most of the major chain stores fled the aging central business district and located at East Hills. The East Belt became the center of St. Joseph's retail growth, following the gradual shifting of population and money away from the inner city to the outskirts of town, a trend throughout the nation. Other smaller shopping centers soon sprang up along the Belt.

Downtown was left with picturesque but mostly vacant relics of the last century when the city was a thriving "blue-collar" commercial center. Facing the reality of urban blight, public and private sectors cooperated to remedy the situation and show pride in their hometown. A multi-million-dollar urban renewal program was launched and approved by the voters in 1970. A Bank Credit Pool was established by the city's financial institutions to assist projects needing financial support. St. Joseph's hospitals expanded to provide medical services not only for the city but also for the entire Midland Empire. Residential areas expanded, new schools, banks and other business buildings were erected.

Work for a four-year college was stepped up, and 1969 saw the new educational institution, Missouri Western College, move into its spacious campus with all-new buildings.

The 1960s may have come in slowly, but they went out swinging.

Reverend Cecil Franks gave out Bibles to the 1960 re-run riders after they had taken Alexander Major's famous Pony Express oath. Photograph by Don Reynolds; courtesy of the St. Joseph Museum

Left to right: Mrs. George Docking, wife of the Governor of Kansas; Congressman William R. Hull of Missouri; Governor Jim Blair of Missouri; and Governor George Docking of Kansas at the Pony Express Centennial. Photograph by Don Reynolds; courtesy of the St. Joseph Museum

The group of white buildings in the upper center of this photograph comprised the St. Joseph State Hospital in 1962. Frederick Avenue runs in front of the buildings and goes east to west. The Belt Highway, running north and south, is in the foreground, and Thirty-Sixth Street, going north and south, is in the center of the picture. Cool Crest Miniature Golf Links is on the Belt Highway to the right of the water tower, and the Pony Express Motel and Restaurant is at the extreme left bottom of the photo. The building with the dome roof was the former home of Skateland, now the location of the People's Furniture Company, and directly east is the Snow White Restaurant. The St. Joseph Driving Range (no longer there) is west of the Water Tower. Photograph courtesy of Strathmann Photography

According to the St. Joseph News–Press (circa 1965), "razing of old buildings, construction of new and remodeling of others is changing the face of St. Joseph. The view is to the northeast and covers the southeast secion of the downtown area. The post office is near the right center. Below it is the new Edmond Plaza Parking area and above it is the new Library Square. The library is above and at the left of the square. At the extreme right is Junior College and to the left of it, its student union building. Frederick Avenue and the city hall appear at the upper left." Photograph by L. C. Shady; courtesy of the St. Joseph News–Press

Industry and entertainment began moving to the eastern edge of the city in the 1960s. The East Hills Shopping Center, ten acres under one roof, Frederick and Belt, opened in 1965. Photograph by Ted Warner

The Whitaker Cable Corporation plant at 3501 Leonard Road. The company started business at a plant on Ninth Street in 1943 and moved to Industrial Park in 1963. Photograph courtesy of the Whitaker Cable Corporation

197

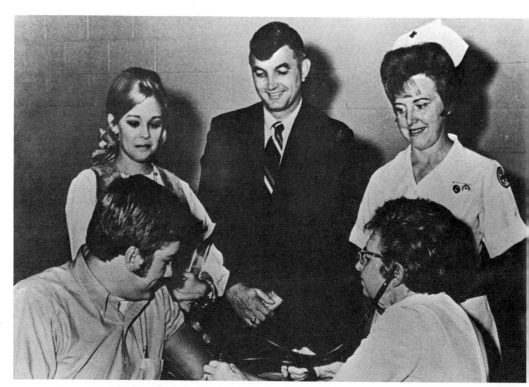

Missouri Western State College students willingly gave their blood for the Vietnam War. Standing, center, is Dr. M.O. Looney, who has been college president since 1967. Photograph courtesy of Missouri Western State College, The Griffon

Fannie Chisholm Hurst and the trail boss are presenting Mayor Douglas Merrifield with a scroll commemorating the one-hundredth anniversary of the trail drive from Cuero, Texas, to St. Joseph, May 4, 1966. Left to right: Clint Coons, president of the Chamber of Commerce; Mrs. Hurst, queen; Henry C. Mills, trail boss; Mayor Douglas Merrifield; Byron Means, vice-president, manager of Pearl Brewing Company, St. Joseph (St. Joseph Museum Graphic). Photograph courtesy of the St. Joseph Museum

Names, faces, and fashions have changed with the growth of Missouri Western State College. In years past, jeans were the exception. Today they are almost a rule. Photograph courtesy of Missouri Western State College, The Griffon

Missouri Western State College's administration building. Today the college is a $25 million plant with the primary campus east of Interstate 29 and north of Mitchell. The west campus is on the west side of Interstate 29 and north of Mitchell.

St. Joseph voters approved establishment of a Missouri Western Junior College in 1965. Under terms of legislation which also became law in 1965, Missouri Western State would provide the facilities and the state would assume the costs of operating and maintaining the third and fourth years of college. In 1966, voters in the Missouri Western State College district approved a general obligation bond issue of $6,055,000 to provide funds for construction of the necessary buildings. In 1968, the board of curators approved establishment of the third and fourth years of college here.

When Missouri Western moved to its new campus in 1969, three buildings were ready for use. They were the Frank S. Popplewell administration/classroom building; the Evan R. Agenstein science/mathematics buildings; and the Warren E. Hearnes Learning Resource Center. Construction of other buildings followed over a period of time. In 1975, the State Assembly approved legislation providing for full funding for the college by the state, effective July 1, 1977. Photograph courtesy of Ival Lawhon, Jr.

Stevens Hat Manufacturing Company, Incorporated, at Whitaker and Leonard Road. In 1969, the company built its 140,000-square-foot plant here in the city's new industrial park. In 1972, the plant was doubled in size. The Stevens Hat Company was founded in St. Joseph in 1917 by Simon Pitluck and Hyman and Harry Rosenthal. Their first hat-making shop was at Third and Felix streets. The next larger shop, at Seventh and Sylvanie, was enlarged and came to take up the entire Seventh Street block from Charles to Sylvanie. The next move was to Industrial Park.

The entire Stetson hat operation in this country was purchased by the owners of Stevens Hat Company is 1970. Stetson hats are known all over the world, so the city of St. Joseph is also recognized because every Stetson made in the United States is made here. Photograph courtesy of the Stevens Hat Manufacturing Company, Incorporated

The Methodist Medical Center, Eighth and Faraon streets. Major remodeling of the main building in 1963 added new equipment and furnishings and brought the hospital to a 320-bed capacity. The Methodist Medical Center's opening of the Pavilion, constructed 1969-1972, made it one of the first hospitals in the nation to offer multi-level care for extended-care patients. The Pavilion has four floors of the latest medical equipment and trained staff members to offer rehabilitation plus extended care to patients suffering from a wide variety of disabilities. Photograph courtesy of Ron Sharp and the Methodist Medical Center

Sylvia Einbender, owner of Einbender's leading women's clothing store, poses with two of her models at a style show in the 1960s. Photograph courtesy of Einbender's

A 1970 view of the northeast corner of Fourth and Edmond streets, showing the Robidoux Apartments, from which Joseph Robidoux's funeral was held. Photograph by Don Reynolds; courtesy of the St. Joseph Museum

chapter 17

The Seventies... and Beyond

The Chamber of Commerce's campaign to "Think Proud" gathered steam in the 1970s. The amount of industrial development has been astounding: since 1968, there have been thirty-four industrial expansions and twenty-one new industry locations. More than 4,000 new manufacturing jobs have been created by the addition of more than 3 million square feet of new manufacturing space. St. Joseph Hospital is constructing a new $25 million hospital on the east side of the city, and Methodist Medical Center is making major additions.

In addition to the industrial expansion, a $50 million West Belt Highway providing an Interstate expressway into the central business district and a new Missouri River Bridge are under contract by the Missouri State Highway Department.

Citizens have rallied behind the improvement projects, approving an annexation proposal which added sixteen square miles and 5,500 population to the city and a bond issue to be used in construction of a $19 million secondary sewage treatment plant. Three new parking lots, providing 1,200 parking spaces in the downtown area, were financed with a $4.55 million general obligation bond in 1975. A bond issue was approved and used to purchase and renovate the old Missouri Theatre and, more recently, another $4 million bond proposal was approved to restore the Buchanan County Court House. Another $4.8 million bond issue was approved by the voters to construct a new Civic Arena in the downtown area to be used for conventions, concerts, shows, and exhibitions. A $7 million, 150-room hotel complex is planned to be constructed adjacent to the Civic Arena.

Downtown has had an attractive facelift. The Land Clearance Redevelopment Authority acquired and demolished most of the substandard structures in the area. A number of remodeling and expansion projects, rebuilding and relocating, took place. Cosmetic alterations such as new storefronts and store signs, awnings, and lights are characteristic. Downtown streets got badly needed paving and repairs.

In December 1977, the one-million-dollar downtown mall, stretching for three blocks along Felix Street, Fifth to Eighth, opened, and culminated the urban renewal program. Retail stores, mainly locally financed, and white-collar banking institutions, government offices, medical facilities, and business complexes make the area one of variety and texture. While realizing downtown will never again be the retail shopping district it once was, the Downtown, Inc., association is confident the new Civic Arena, hotel, and West Belt will bring renewed interest to the inner city, especially a resurgence of night life. Also, there is a movement toward increased residential development in the downtown area. Older homes, often the only affordable ones, are being bought and renovated. Apartments are being built in upper areas of some central city buildings. More housing for the elderly is being constructed on downtown fringes.

St. Joseph has one of the richest collections of late nineteenth and early twentieth century architecture in the region. While the urban renewal demolition leveled some buildings which the history-conscious wanted to save, a number of historic structures have been preserved. The more-than-a-century-old court house, for example, is being restored to its nineteenth-century splendor. Other earlier examples are the Bank of the State of Missouri, now the Missouri Valley Trust Company, and the German American Bank restored by the First Federal Savings and Loan Association.

Candace Grenier (now Mrs. Craig Spangler) was one of many Missouri Western State College students who cast their first vote in the '70s. Eighteen-year-olds were granted the right to vote with the passage of the Twenty-Sixth Amendment in 1971. Photograph courtesy of Missouri Western State College, The Griffon

The Woolco Department Store, 1417 North Belt, opened for business in 1971. Photograph courtesy of the Woolco Department Store

Emphasis is now being placed not only on restoring the old structures' charm but also on functionalizing it to meet late twentieth century needs. Earlier illustrations of this trend were the Tootle home which became the St. Joseph Museum, the Patee House, and the Jesse James Home which also are now museums. More recently, the Geiger House, built in 1911, has been redesigned into a modern banking facility. Wholesale Row, buildings of the former booming wholesale industry, is undergoing renovation for use as offices, stores, and restaurants. Robidoux Row, when restored, will become a picturesque tourist attraction.

The result is an intriguing, charming city of contrasts—the old and the new learning to co-exist, the elegance of the past complementing the emerging revitalization, looking ahead to the future.

And what does the future hold for St. Joseph? Traditionally conservative, the city's mood is one of guarded optimism. With a livestock market which is still sixth largest in the nation, the city continues to be involved to its rolled-up shirtsleeves in agriculture. And agriculture keeps a positive attitude regarding the future as long as there are hungry mouths to feed. But, more importantly, St. Joseph is now an industrially diversified city, with energy and transportation sources readily available, superior municipal services, clean air and water, open spaces, and a parkway system that is the envy of the nation.

The city is large enough to compete with larger municipalities in services and facilities, yet small enough to be known as the city with the friendly personality. Natives stop and say "Hi!" to newcomers they meet on the street, take time to answer their questions, help them get settled in. People *like* to live here. And where people like to live, industries like to locate.

Standing on the threshold of the new decade, we can only speculate what the future holds. The only certainty is that changes will occur, that high tides and low tides will come to our town as surely and relentlessly as the Missouri River continues to flow past our waterfront. But St. Joseph has experienced reverses before, has bounced back, and has acquired resiliency. Along with its conservative bearing, there is a positive attitude of confidence. Come what may, St. Joseph can handle it.

The 1973-74 Missouri Western State College Basketball Team played in the NAIA National Tournament in Kansas City to close out the most exciting basketball season in Griffon history to that date. The Western cagers, under Head Coach Gary Filbert, finished the season with a 25-6 mark and a twelfth place national ranking among small college teams, and a first place district rating by the Carr Rating Service. Led by a powerful front line of Mark and Jeff Brown and Geoff Roberts, the Griffon roundballers grabbed better than 61 percent of the total rebounds to rank first in the nation in rebounding. Photograph courtesy of Missouri Western State College, The Griffon

The St. Joseph Symphony performs from the stage of the Missouri Theatre, 1974. The conductor is Dr. Russell T. Waite. Photograph courtesy of the Allied Arts Council of St. Joseph, Missouri, Incorporated

View westward from the Corby-
Forsee Building on Felix Street
toward the Missouri River and
Kansas. Market Square row is at left
center (1971). Photograph by Don
Reynolds; courtesy of the St. Joseph
Museum

THE FIRST NATIONAL BANK

The United Missouri Bank of St. Joseph, Twenty-Fifth Street and Frederick Avenue. The original structure was built in 1912 for Dr. Jacob Geiger, a German emigrant and a prominent St. Joseph physician. Among other distinctions, Dr. Geiger once assisted at a cataract operation on Joseph Robidoux and performed the Jesse James post mortem. The Geiger home was sold in 1941, and, for a while, housed an antique shop. In 1976, the banking facility bought the property, renovated it, and converted the mansion into a bank building. They not only preserved the decor, often working around difficult structural problems to save the carved beams, bricks, and baseboards, but added touches to recreate the decor, the mood, and the lighting of the early nineteenth-century era. The inlaid parquetry floor and the chandelier in the original living room are still there. So is the original front door. When the four drive-in windows were added, care was taken to match the arrangement and styling of the bricks used to build them. Period art lamps light the parking lot. Photograph by Ival Lawhon, Jr.

Instructor James R. Hayes (St. Joseph Chief of Police) and Craig Spangler demonstrate the correct procedure for fingerprinting to the Criminalistics class at Missouri Western State College. To meet the growing needs of the students and the community, a greater emphasis is being placed upon career programs at the college. These one- and-two-year programs provide challenging alternatives to the four-year degree. Photograph courtesy of Missouri Western State College, The Griffon

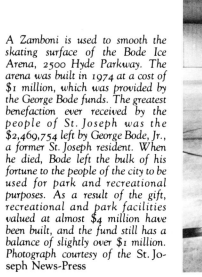

A Zamboni is used to smooth the skating surface of the Bode Ice Arena, 2500 Hyde Parkway. The arena was built in 1974 at a cost of $1 million, which was provided by the George Bode funds. The greatest benefaction ever received by the people of St. Joseph was the $2,469,754 left by George Bode, Jr., a former St. Joseph resident. When he died, Bode left the bulk of his fortune to the people of the city to be used for park and recreational purposes. As a result of the gift, recreational and park facilities valued at almost $4 million have been built, and the fund still has a balance of slightly over $1 million. Photograph courtesy of the St. Joseph News-Press

The "Balloon Man," a familiar
figure at the Apple Blossom parades,
displays his wares at the 1977
parade. Photograph by Ival
Lawhon, Jr.

The last Mayor's Christmas Party for the children is held at the old city auditorium in 1977. Photograph by Ival Lawhon, Jr.

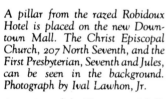

A pillar from the razed Robidoux Hotel is placed on the new Downtown Mall. The Christ Episcopal Church, 207 North Seventh, and the First Presbyterian, Seventh and Jules, can be seen in the background. Photograph by Ival Lawhon, Jr.

A portion of the Downtown Mall, Seventh and Felix streets. Photograph by Ival Lawhon, Jr.

The American National Bank had owned the Hotel Robidoux since 1970 and had it demolished June 13, 1976. Ground-breaking ceremonies for a new bank site were soon held, and two years later the new building was completed. Photograph courtesy of Robidoux Center

210

Opening ceremonies of the NAIA World Series are held at Phil Welch Stadium, Twenty-Fifth and Commercial streets, in 1978. Photograph by Ival Lawhon, Jr.

The altar from the former Saints Peter and Paul Church, Twentieth and Messanie, was moved to the Queen of the Apostles church, 507 South Tenth, in 1978. The building at Twentieth and Messanie Street is now vacant and is for sale. Photograph by Ival Lawhon, Jr.

A Rathskellar Disco became a regular event by popular demand at Missouri Western State College in 1978. "On the wings of Saturday Night Fever, the disco had arrived. Thursday night discos became as popular as the Wednesday night trips to Kansas City. The pulsating beat found its place at the Fall Icebreaker, right through to the Spring Dance. The dress ranged from T-shirts and jeans to formals" (Carol Mabry, The Griffon). Photograph courtesy of Missouri Western State College, The Griffon

Robidoux Center, the modern, multimillion-dollar, six-story office building was developed by the owner, Kroh Brothers of Kansas City, on the site of the old Hotel Robidoux. Robidoux Center is the new home of the American National Bank.

Robidoux Center was dedicated May 20, 1978 at a public open house. Visitors toured the building, which holds many artifacts of the old Robidoux Hotel. Photograph courtesy of Robidoux Center

The Seventies...
And Beyond

The 1978 St. Joseph City Council is sworn in by City Clerk Walter T. Welsh. From left to right: Jim Connors, Larry Koch, John Lucas, Leroy Maxwell, Steve Nikes, Dave Polsky, Jim Sollars, Mike Welsh, and Joanne Youngdahl. Photograph by Ival Lawhon, Jr.

Aerial photo of the I-229 West Belt construction in 1978, from the south, looking north. The Missouri River is at the left. Photograph by Ival Lawhon, Jr.

Shadows falling on the West Belt construction in the southern part of the city make barber poles of the piers. Photograph by Ival Lawhon, Jr.

The Marine Corps 'Harrier' lands at Rosecrans Memorial Airport in 1979. Photograph by Ival Lawhon, Jr.

The Frank Holder Dance Company performed jointly with the St. Joseph Public Schools in connection with the Artists-in-Schools program at the Missouri Theatre, November 15, 1979. Photograph courtesy of the Missouri Arts Council

Gordon Wiser, Mayor of St. Joseph, welcomes 4-H'ers and friends to the 1979 Interstate Show held at East Hills Mall. Located in the heart of the nation's rich farmlands and livestock-raising areas, St. Joseph annually hosts the Interstate Show, which attracts exhibitors and participants from three states. Photograph courtesy of the Missouri University Extension Center, St. Joseph, Missouri

At the Chuckwagon Day Camp, 1974, held at Camp Geiger near St. Joseph, children learned about food and its importance to good health. Other activities included crafts, recreation, and swimming. Photograph courtesy of the University of Missouri Extension Center, St. Joseph, Missouri and Strathmann Photography

The St. Joseph Historical Society
celebrated Joseph Robidoux's birth-
day, August 10, 1979, by dining in
the courtyard of Robidoux Row, the
apartment complex built by St. Joseph's founder about 1850. The
Historical Society is making restoration of Robidoux Row one of their
most important projects. In 1974,
they purchased the property, then a
dilapidated shell of a building, and
held a weed-pulling party to launch
the project. The first step in the
restoration program was to hire an
architect to plan the details. Phases I
and II of the project focused on
preparation and research, the building of a rock retaining wall, recon-
struction of the sloping cedar roof,
and the installation of guttering and
dormers. Phase III includes paving
the courtyard, rebuilding the walls
and floors, replacing windows, and
landscaping. Five Living History
Rooms are being restored and furnished to protray Robidoux and his
times authentically. When the
restoration is completed, it is hoped
Robidoux Row will become a popular tourist attraction. It is listed in
the National Register of Historic
Places. Photograph courtesy of the
St. Joseph News-Press; photograph by Ival Lawhon, Jr.

A giant American flag flew over the
rededication ceremony August 20,
1979 at the 106-year-old Buchanan
County Court House. A parade from
City Hall preceded the event, mark-
ed by speeches by the Chief Justice of
the Missouri Supreme Court, John
Bardgett, and the Governor of
Missouri, Joseph Teasdale. County
court houses have stood on the
present site since the land was
donated for that purpose by St. Joseph founder Joseph Robidoux 133
years ago. Every Missouri Governor
and United States Senator has
campaigned at the court house.
President Harry S Truman was a
frequent visitor to the building. The
men who killed Jesse James stood
trial and pleaded guilty in the
Buchanan County Court House.
Photograph courtesy of the St. Joseph News-Press and Strathmann
Photography

St. Joseph city officials participated in the Southwest Parkway Viaduct opening in June 1980. Demolition of the old bridge had started in 1979. The 520-foot-long bridge, which was originally built in the 1920s at the time the city's boulevard system was expanded, carries Southwest Boulevard traffic across Garfield Avenue and the Burlington Northern and Santa Fe railroad tracks. Photograph courtesy of the St. Joseph News-Press and Strathmann Photography

St. Joseph's new Civic Arena, Fourth and Felix streets, opened in November 1980. Photograph by Ival Lawhon, Jr.

The expanse of the I-229 project unfolds through the western part of the city. This view is to the north with the Pony Express bridge on the left. The piers for the new Missouri River bridge are visible. The railroad bridge is in the open position to the north. The riverfront portion of the I-229 Highway can be seen following the curve of the river at the top of the photograph. Photograph by Ival Lawhon, Jr.

215

An aerial photograph of St. Joseph in the early 1980s reveals an interesting and picturesque blending of the old and the new. The view is to the northeast. The Missouri River is at the bottom of the picture. The new I-229 West Belt construction runs along the river. The Corby building, in the fifth block of Felix, is the tall building in the center of the picture. The new Downtown Mall runs from Fifth to Eighth Street on Felix. The new Civic Arena is the block-wide white building behind and to the left of the Corby building. Robidoux Center is the building above and to the left of the Civic Arena.

The more than century-old Buchanan County Court House is the building with the dome to the left of Robidoux Center. The Landmark building, Fourth and Jules, is below the court house in the picture. The Missouri Valley Trust building, oldest bank building west of the Mississippi River, is below the Corby building, at Fourth and Felix. Photograph by Ival Lawhon, Jr.

217

Bibliography

Chapman, Carl, and Eleanor. *Indians and Archaeology of Missouri*. Columbia: Univ. of Missouri Press, 1964.

Doherty, Mary Lee. *St. Joseph Magazine*. St. Joseph, 1977.

Faubion, Hazel. *Tales of Old "St. Joe" and The Frontier Days*. Cassville, Mo.: Litho Printers, 1977.

Foley, William. *A History of Missouri*. Vols. I and II. Columbia, Mo.: Univ. of Missouri Press, 1971.

Griffon, The. St. Joseph, Missouri Western State College.

Hall, Ben M. *The Best Remaining Seats*. New York: C. N. Potter, 1961.

Illustrated Review of St. Joseph, Missouri. C. H. Dunn and Company, 1887.

Lilly, Seward. *History of Buchanan County, 1881*. Cassville, Mo.: Litho Printers, 1973.

Logan, Sheridan. *Old Saint Jo, Gateway to the West, 1799-1932*. Lunenburg, Vt.: The Stinehour Press, 1979.

New Comers' Key to St. Joseph. St. Joseph: Courtesy of Townsend and Wall, 1941.

Pictorial St. Joseph. St. Joseph: Journal of Commerce, Pictorial Publishing Company. 1911.

Popplewell, Frank. *Fiftieth Anniversary of St. Joseph Junior College*. St. Joseph, 1965.

St. Joseph, Missouri, as a Center for the Cattle Trade. St. Joseph, 1937.

Rutt, Chris. *History of Buchanan County and the City of Saint Joseph*. Chicago: Biographical Publishing Company, 1904.

St. Joseph and Northwest Missouri. Illustrated Souvenir Edition of the St. Joseph Daily News. St. Joseph, circa 1894.

St. Joseph, Missouri, Today. Chamber of Commerce booklet. St. Joseph, 1927.

St. Joseph Museum Graphics. St. Joseph Museum. St. Joseph, Missouri.

St. Joseph News-Press and Gazette. St. Joseph, Missouri.

Show Me. St. Joseph: Union Terminal Railways, 1923.

Travelers' Souvenir Illustrated. Souvenir booklet of the United Commercial Travelers of America. St. Joseph: Combe Printing Company, 1897.

Utz, Nellie. *History of the Growth and Development of Saint Joseph*. St. Joseph, 1935.

Views of St. Joseph, Missouri, Today. St. Joseph: Combe Printing Company, 1897.

Index

Missouri native Mildred Grenier, well-known freelance writer, has lived in St. Joseph more than thirty years. She is the author of ten published books, numerous magazine articles, and a television play. A former school teacher, she taught creative writing in the Continuing Education department at Missouri Western State College.